"This book is tremendous. I couldn't stop reading. An elegantly simple framework and a seriously smart book."

—**STEPHEN M. R. COVEY,** bestselling author, *The Speed of Trust*

"Whitney Johnson has few equals when it comes to the topic of personal growth. And now she's written a true masterpiece. Her model is instructive and straightforward, but that's the least of it. I love, love, love the case studies. The people she's visited with and the stories they've given her deserve the word 'peerless.' Yes, it's a serious study, but it's also a true, genuine page-turner."

—**TOM PETERS,** bestselling coauthor, *In Search of Excellence*

"Johnson offers a clear philosophical framework and actionable advice on how to love our lives and do our best work, along with wonderful stories that show us what she means. I loved this book!"

—**KIM SCOTT,** *New York Times* bestselling author, *Radical Candor* and
   Just Work

"This is a groundbreaking book in a class by itself. It hooked me with the first sentence, and it kept getting more intriguing from there. You and I are designed to grow, to keep bringing more of ourselves to the surface. Johnson takes the reader on a journey that begins with a deep longing to grow and ends having taken us beyond our limiting beliefs to a state of inner freedom and perpetual new beginnings. *Smart Growth* is required reading for anyone interested in growing a company in the most satisfying ways."

—**BOB PROCTOR,** bestselling author, *You Were Born Rich*

"*Smart Growth* is a brilliant and beautifully written book. The stories are so compelling that you can almost miss their solid foundation of good science and business acumen. Johnson is a collector of wisdom, and she generously shares what she's collected. She guides us to where we want to go even if we were afraid to go there. *Smart Growth* is good for you, your team, and your business. I loved it, and you will too."

—**CAROL KAUFFMAN,** founder, Institute of Coaching, Harvard Medical
   School; Senior Leadership Advisor, Egon Zehnder

"Whitney Johnson brilliantly demystifies the process of growth by showing us not only how to start something new but also how to keep going, even when it's tough. Exceptional stories make *Smart Growth* a delight to read. Actionable insights make it essential for business leaders who want to grow their companies."

—**VALA AFSHAR,** Chief Digital Evangelist, Salesforce

"If I were a CEO, I'd want every one of my leaders to read this human, engaging, and realistic book about building high-performance, high-growth teams."

—**RITA McGRATH,** Professor, Columbia Business School;
Fellow, Strategic Management Society; and bestselling author,
Seeing Around Corners

"There are so many memorable concepts and inspiring stories in *Smart Growth,* I can't pick a favorite. By the end you'll be ready to learn and grow both yourself and your organization in ways you may not yet have imagined. This book is a powerful reminder that the fundamental unit of growth and change in our ecosystem is each one of us."

—**MELISSA WERNECK,** Global Chief People Officer, Kraft Heinz

"I always learn from Whitney Johnson. *Smart Growth* examines the often-overlooked intersection between the growth of individuals and the growth of organizations. It offers valuable insights, whether you're looking to take on new challenges or successfully lead a diverse team."

—**JUSTIN OSOFSKY,** Chief Operating Officer, Instagram

"Growth and change can often feel frustrating and slow, both for ourselves and our businesses. Whitney Johnson's expert advice in *Smart Growth* changes this! Full of powerful stories, research, and thoughtful insights, this book will arm you with all you need to grow successfully. A must-read!"

—**MARSHALL GOLDSMITH,** bestselling author, *Triggers, Mojo,*
and *What Got You Here Won't Get You There*

"It seems like everything is smart these days—phones, watches, TVs, refrigerators. Learning and growth are now smart too, with Whitney Johnson's latest book. *Smart Growth* will transform your view of learning—for me it has already opened up an exciting new way to think about growth and development. In fact, this book may be the smartest product of all!"

—**JAMES M. CITRIN,** Leader, Spencer Stuart North American CEO Practice; coauthor, *Leading at a Distance*

"Johnson has written a profound book full of sound advice and great stories to help you master learning and growth. Most authors would stop there, but she masterfully takes her blueprint further, showing you how to help others master their learning and growth, too. Simply genius. Brava!"

—**NANCY DUARTE,** CEO, Duarte, Inc.; bestselling author, *slide:ology* and *Resonate*

SMART GROWTH

SMART GROWTH

How to Grow
Your People to Grow
Your Company

WHITNEY JOHNSON

HARVARD BUSINESS REVIEW PRESS

BOSTON, MASSACHUSETTS

The web addresses referenced in this book were live and correct at the time of the book's publication but may be subject to change.

Library of Congress Cataloging-in-Publication Data is forthcoming.

ISBN: 978-1-64782-115-9
eISBN: 978-1-64782-116-6

The paper used in this publication meets the requirements of the American National Standard for Permanence of Paper for Publications and Documents in Libraries and Archives Z39.48-1992.

To Clayton Christensen—for making this S Curve possible.

Contents

Introduction

[We] each live thousands of lives, for each day we become someone
slightly different. [We] don't change in one giant leap, but across a
million little steps. The most important step a person can take is
always the next one.

—BRANDON SANDERSON

Growth is our default setting.

Astrid Tuminez was born into circumstances that looked like a dead
end.[1] The sixth of seven children, her family moved when she was two
from a remote farming village in the Philippines to the violent slums of the
provincial capital, Iloilo City. Her father made $50 per month. When Tumi-
nez was five, her mother left, leaving her fifteen-year-old sister Marley in
charge. They lived in a bamboo-floored hut on stilts over the sea. There was
no running water, sanitation, or electricity. Marley washed their clothes by
hand. They cooked their meals—primarily rice—on a dirt stove with wood.
When I interviewed Tuminez for the *Disrupt Yourself* podcast she told me,
"I remember having to cook rice at five to six years old, and I was afraid
I would burn our hut down." On the rare occasions when they could buy a
chicken, Marley would butcher it herself and cook it over an open fire. She
caramelized sweetened condensed milk to make a candy called *yema* that
her siblings sold at school—a good source of occasional extra cash.

Nuns from the Catholic order Daughters of Charity invited Tuminez and her sisters to attend a special school for underprivileged children. Initially at the bottom of her class, far behind the other students academically, Tuminez was assigned the last seat, in the last row of the classroom. "That's where the dumbest child sat," she says. She worked ferociously to finish her first school year at the top of her class, "to sit right in front." She says, "I learned to read. I learned to do numbers. I was exposed to this whole world of learning. . . . It was a fairytale." In her school library, she pored over books about faraway, exotic destinations like New York. Tuminez dared to dream that she would live there one day.

Few, if any (except possibly Tuminez), would have imagined that she would someday graduate from Harvard (MA in soviet studies) and MIT (PhD in political science), speak Russian impeccably, become an executive at Microsoft, and preside over an American university with more than forty thousand students—among other distinguished achievements.

I first met Tuminez when she was living and working in the city she had dared to dream about—New York. She had just finished a Kennedy School fellowship in Moscow, working with senior reformers who had helped tear down the Berlin Wall—people like Eduard Shevardnadze and Mikhail Gorbachev. Here was an individual who was indefatigable, unswerving in her determination.

I was in awe.

My wonder then was fleeting. But after a serendipitous encounter with Tuminez in the Boston Airport several years ago, I asked myself the question, "What animates Astrid Tuminez?"

Having since interviewed her in-depth, I now know she is driven to achieve her potential. There is a yearning, deep-bellied, to learn and grow.

Like Tuminez, you and I came into this world preprogrammed to progress. We have different circumstances and curiosities, but the same drive. To want to grow is human. But life has a way of muffling our innate desire to learn. As adults, we often find ourselves stagnant or bored at work and in our personal lives.

If you're reading this book, you are motivated to change and make progress. But maybe you don't know where to start or you believe you can't start. Perhaps you're curious and motivated to grow, but also too overextended with existing obligations to believe you can succeed at something new. Or maybe you have started but want to grow faster still.

Perhaps you want to help the people around you grow. You are a manager looking to decode talent development and succession planning, or a C-suite executive trying to expand your organization's top line. This book is for you too.

But because the fundamental unit of growth in any organization is the individual, our starting point for talking about growth is you.

Some of the questions we will answer are:

- Why, despite the desire to learn, can it be so difficult to start something new and stick with it?

- What does it take to gain and maintain momentum?

- Once we've made considerable progress, why do we sometimes tire of what we're doing and even feel we can no longer do it? Why do we outgrow things so quickly?

The more you understand about your deep longing to grow and how to grow yourself, the greater your capacity to grow your people, to grow your company. That's smart growth.

The S Curve of Learning: A Model for Smart Growth

In the early aughts I met the gentle giant, six-foot-eight Harvard professor Clayton Christensen and was introduced to *disruptive innovation*. This theory—that a Goliath-like legacy business could be overtaken by a silly little David—changed my thinking as a Wall Street equity analyst. It also revolutionized my thinking about growth. By 2004, I had been an award-winning analyst for nearly eight years. I loved it, but I felt like there was something more. After an especially discouraging conversation with my manager, who wanted me to stay right where I was, I had a flash of insight. My current equity analyst self was the incumbent—Goliath. My future self was the upstart—David. To wake up the giant, I had to disrupt myself. It was revelatory: disruption isn't just about products, but about people. If we are willing to step back from who we are, we can slingshot into who we want to be—who people need us to be.

I codified a seven-point framework of Personal Disruption in a 2012 *Harvard Business Review* article and then again in my 2015 book, *Disrupt Yourself*.[2] The gist is this: companies don't disrupt, people do. When we commit to the practice of deliberate self-innovation (that is, Personal Disruption), we accelerate organizational growth. My 2018 title *Build an A-Team* teaches how to leverage the power of Personal Disruption to build winning teams.[3]

I have now studied, written, advised, and coached about human potential for nearly twenty years. This book is the next step. Some people are intuitively proactive in directing their own growth, but even they can benefit when the process is made explicit. A map can jumpstart a smart growth journey. The S Curve of Learning is that map.

The S Curve of Learning

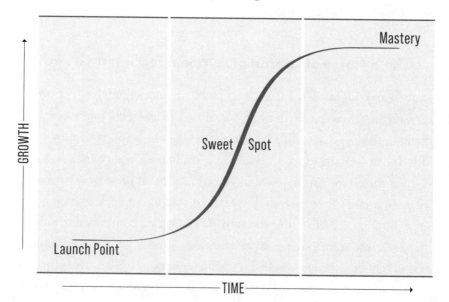

A little background on S Curves: in the 1950s, Iowan and social science researcher E. M. Rogers's PhD dissertation posed the question, "Why did farmers [in his home community] delay for several years in adopting new ideas that could have profited them?"

He found that the rate of adoption of any new idea is S-shaped. The initial rollout is slow, represented by the base of the S. If adoption reaches 10 to 15 percent, what had been considered novel will now be considered worthy of imitation. This is the tipping point of the curve; beyond it, the diffusion of an idea can be impossible to halt. Adoption is rapid through this steep back-of-the-S sweet spot, until about 90 percent saturation is achieved. With little room left to influence change, the pace of adoption slows dramatically.

What Rogers regards as the seminal diffusion study still perfectly illustrates this phenomenon.[4] In 1928, a type of hybrid corn was introduced in Iowa that yielded an increased harvest of 20 percent, was drought resistant, and was better suited to mechanical harvesting. It took five years for the first 10 percent of farmers to adopt this innovation. But then adoption took off, shooting up to 40 percent in the next three years. Then, as there were fewer farmers remaining to adopt, adoption leveled off. Slowly, then quickly, this new seed "ushered in the agricultural innovations beginning in the 1930s that led to a revolution in farm productivity."

The groundbreaking insight for Rogers was that this type of adoption wasn't bound by the type of innovation, "but that the diffusion of innovations was a kind of universal process for social change."

Which brings me to another important insight: the S Curve can also help us penetrate the science of how we grow.[5] The same model that explains how human *groups* change is a meaningful analogue for how *individuals* change. There is still research to be done, but findings in biology, psychology, and neuroscience, along with our qualitative data, support my hypothesis: the S Curve of Learning is a microcosm of the diffusion curve.

The S Curve of Learning models personal growth. Every new skill learned, every challenge faced, takes the form of a distinct learning curve. We can pinpoint where we are in the growth process; we can decide what our next step needs to be. We can use this model to self-direct our growth; we can use it to help others grow.

When you finish reading this book you will have a clear mental map of how human growth is accomplished. This will increase your capacity to grow—yourself and others.

The Six Stages of Growth

This book primarily follows the S Curve, from the Launch Point of an S Curve (chapters 1 and 2), through the Sweet Spot (chapters 3 and 4), and into Mastery (chapters 5 and 6). We'll diagram the six stages of growth you encounter along the S Curve in the six chapters of these three sections. They are Explorer, Collector, Accelerator, Metamorph, Anchor, and Mountaineer. The S Curve framework will guide you as you move forward, deliberately and autonomously accelerating your growth. A seventh chapter, Ecosystem, examines the environment needed to expedite growth.

At the end of each major section, there will be detailed takeaways for organizational leaders. This is where we will be tactical, providing you with specific ways to apply this model, including how to use our S Curve Insight Platform.[6]

Each phase of the S Curve of Learning is marked by its own distinctive characteristics, frustrations, and thrills. When we start something new, we are at the launch point, grasping for knowledge. New behaviors are not yet our modus operandi (and like farmers in Iowa, we don't know if we want them to be). Because part of our brain (the prefrontal cortex) is processing the new and trying to understand how the new connects with the old, it has limited processing capacity. Our brain can easily get overloaded.

At the launch point, there are many new opportunities we can pursue. I call this the *Explorer* phase (chapter 1). We are a thrill-seeking species—and what can be more thrilling than standing at the precipice of becoming more of our own person? We may go headlong into this honeymoon of learning. Jubilant. We may also be awkward and unsure—anxious, impatient, apprehensive. With so much pending and uncertain, we can experience this phase as *slow*.

The Stages of Growth

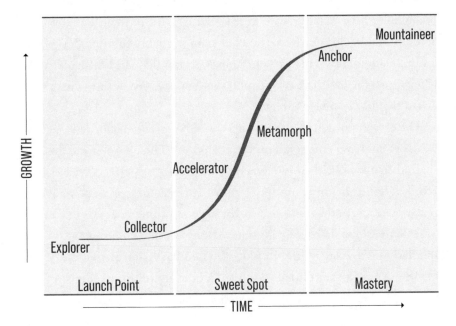

Once we decide an S Curve merits further evaluation, we become a *Collector* (chapter 2), seeking input, feedback, and data that will help us assess the fit and value of a particular curve. It might still be a slog. It's *slow*, but it will also help us *grow*.

Once we reach the tipping point (assuming we reach it), we gain momentum up the rising slope of the S Curve. This is the sweet spot (part 2). What is new hasn't yet become a natural part of us, so deliberate practice is still the order of the day. But because we are gaining confidence that we can become who we set out to be, hope swells as our growth accelerates. We are an *Accelerator* (chapter 3). We experience *fast* growth.

As we focus on doing something new, we are forging a new identity. What we do becomes who we are. It's now natural and reflexive. We've conquered the change-averse instinct within us. Now we are a *Metamorph* (chapter 4). A lot of growth is achieved in a little time. Effort is still essential, but as our brain picks up the pace connecting the new with the old, growth accelerates and becomes difficult, if not impossible, to stop. It's exhilarating and feels *faster* than before.

At the high end of the S Curve, ease displaces effort, and we are in the mastery phase (part 3). We have reached our objective and maximized potential growth. Whatever we were learning to do, or to be, has now been accomplished. This newly learned behavior is anchored in us. It is effortless and automatic. What was once novel, unfamiliar, and difficult can be labeled pro forma: the new normal, the new *you*. We declare victory, we are in the *Anchor* phase (chapter 5).

The caveat: once the skill we've mastered has become effortless, we have excess mental and emotional processing power. The new neurons are now the old neurons. We no longer enjoy the feel-good effects of learning. Exhilaration can wane, and our brains can become bored. *Slow.* We all reach plateaus, and it's a praiseworthy accomplishment. It was hard work to scale the slope, hard enough that we may be reluctant to move on. But stagnation is a waste of life. In time, the familiar lethargy that goaded us to climb an S Curve returns. We need a new mountain to climb, a fresh S Curve of Learning. We become a *Mountaineer* (chapter 6).

How Growth Happens

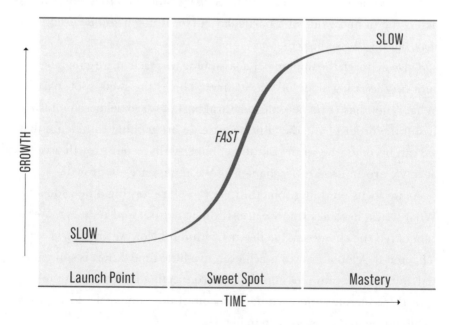

Nobody climbs their S Curve alone. We need guidance and support from our environment. This is the growth *Ecosystem*: the web of interpersonal relationships that makes growth possible (chapter 7). Ecosystems are not an afterthought. We can have a map to guide our growth, and a backpack of tools, but if the weather is unfavorable, we may be thwarted in our journey.

The S Curve of Learning is a map to look at your life: where you were, where you are, and where you want to go—a continuous pathway to achieving potential. When you can picture yourself moving along this growth curve, you can more easily plan a trajectory and plot your progress. You can get smart about your growth.

A Model of Smart Growth

Here's how it works in actual practice. Harry Kraemer is the former chief executive of the health-care giant Baxter International and now a professor of leadership at the Kellogg School of Management. In early 2021, after learning about our model, he talked to me about his own career as a series of S Curves.[7] "The first phase," he told me, "was when I was in seventh or eighth grade, and taking my religious obligations very seriously." The S Curves we choose are usually motivated by our values; the Kraemer family's values were centered on their Catholic faith. Young Harry thought he might become a priest like the uncle he looked up to, Father Francis. Knowing Harry well, Father Francis encouraged him to take time to explore: to catalog his abilities and look at different avenues for a values-driven life. Ministers, priests, and rabbis can have a big impact on their congregants, Francis said, but that was just one of many spiritual paths. It was important for Harry to look at what he did well, and discover how he could best serve as a force for good.

Kraemer took this to heart, took a pass on divinity school, and attended the Kellogg School of Management instead. Math was his best subject in school, so he studied accounting. Though Harry never became a priest, he cites this experience as his first important S Curve: making that pivotal decision about where his life would lead. This will happen with many of our S Curves: we start by exploring the curve itself. Some we will commit to, others we will not, but in all cases the decision-making process is a journey within our journey.

After graduating from Kellogg, Kraemer took an entry-level junior analyst position at Baxter International. Math led to accounting and that led to finance and mergers and acquisitions (M&A). Harry decided, "I'm going to really focus on M&A. I'm going to be the best M&A guy." He demonstrated early aptitude on projects handed to him by Baxter's CFO and CEO. "I've got this wired," he thought. "I'm locked in. I feel really good." He told me, "I was starting to feel comfortable."

But comfort wasn't in the cards. Disruption was. The CFO said to him, "I think there are other things you could be doing. You seem like you could manage people and teams." Kraemer didn't jump at the chance. "That's kind of out of my comfort zone," he told his CFO. The CFO's response: "Good leaders don't want to get comfortable. I think you ought to get into a division and work your way up."

Kraemer was starting out on another launch point of a new S Curve. He was no longer in corporate, but one face in one division in a sea of twenty-two divisions. What were his odds of standing out? Kraemer's previous objective was to be the best M&A guy. Now he wanted to be the best divisional guy. Kraemer says he was fortunate, surrounded by great people, a supportive ecosystem that helped him gain competence. Running small divisions turned into running big divisions, upward progress on his new S Curve of leadership. "This is good," he described thinking. "I'm getting happy again. I'm getting organized. I can start to kind of coast."

In this book we'll learn why starting to coast is a bad idea: comfort zones are the bane of growth. Kraemer was lucky to have Father Francis, and Baxter's former CFO, and then the CEO, push him to disrupt himself. The CEO told him, "You have a financial background. I think you could be the next CFO."

It had been twelve years since Kraemer had been in finance. He had a major knowledge gap: he didn't know tax rules. Again, out of his comfort zone, on to the launch point of a new S Curve of Learning. He gained competence, accelerated into the sweet spot, and saw mastery within reach at the top of the "best CFO" S Curve.

Then he got a call from the board. They were considering Kraemer for a job he hadn't sought—CEO. Kraemer was initially cautious as he had been with each S Curve jump. Being a math guy, he takes calculated risks. The consistent factors in his calculations are: 1) can I learn and grow; 2) can I add value; 3) will it be fun? He wasn't sure the reward of this change would be worth the risk (a subject we'll address in the first chapter). But three voices urged him to accept the challenge. The board thought he could thrive in the role. His wife, Julie, thought he could too. Then Julie invoked the voice of Father Francis, reminding Kraemer of the seminal conversation from his childhood: catalog your gifts, explore many avenues, use your best gifts to influence for good. What a tremendous opportunity, Julie said to him, to be influencing fifty-five thousand people.

Meanwhile there were five people whose smart growth was more urgent to Kraemer than all fifty-five thousand Baxter employees: his children. Parenthood is a towering S Curve of Learning, and it ran parallel to Kraemer's career. All five kids needed one-on-one leadership. Could Kraemer help Baxter grow when his number one priority was at home?

Kraemer took the CEO job, but not without trepidation. That's how it feels to be at the launch point of a new S Curve. When he handed off the reins five years later, he'd been at Baxter twenty-three years. Passing through a season of struggle, Baxter had lost its stature and credibility in the financial markets. As a man who strives to live his values, Kraemer accepted responsibility for the failures and acknowledged that a fresh perspective was needed at the helm.[8] He bumped himself from the top of his S Curve. Still young, he wondered if it was time to find another company to run. He again thought, "I've got this wired. Even if it's not a $13 billion company, I could start at $5 billion. I've got the playbook."

He was out of Baxter less than a week when he was nudged in a new direction. Don Jacobs was dean emeritus at Kellogg and Kraemer's former finance professor. Jacobs said, "I want you to teach."

Kraemer responded, "'You mean have a syllabus, grade papers? That's not happening. I run companies.'" Jacobs's response: "You've already done that. If God's given you more time, why would you run another company?"

Kraemer opted to teach. Jacobs assumed Kraemer would teach finance, his strong subject. But Harry wanted to focus on leadership instead: values and ethics. The boy who thought he might lead a spiritual flock has become the man who teaches values to a flock of future business leaders.

Harry Kraemer's career so far is a perfect example of smart growth when mapped to the S Curve model. Each curve has been related to the last but never identical. Each curve was a challenge, a disruption. And each curve has shared a common denominator in its objective: be the best. The best M&A guy, best divisional guy, best CFO, best CEO, best teacher, best father and husband, best Christian he knew how to be. The mastery Kraemer seeks at the top of the overarching S Curve of his life is growth for himself and for others. Kraemer summarizes, "Leadership has nothing to do with titles and organizational charts. . . . It's about developing people." Smart growth will help you do that.

Harry Kraemer's story, and other stories we'll share, demonstrate that the S Curve of Learning is not a mere abstraction. It is a powerful tool that can maximize growth when applied in any life and any organization. Significant progress—whether in your career, in your team members, in your company, or in your personal life—can be visually represented by a rising S-shaped curve, like a wave one rides from novice to master, novelty to familiarity. We can apply this model deliberately. We can use it to develop a smart growth career, build a smart growth company, live a smart growth life.

Grow or Don't Grow. You Choose

Contrast the stories of Astrid Tuminez and Harry Kraemer with this letter to "Dear Abby," America's popular newspaper advice column:

> Dear Abby, . . . Life has me worn out. I have accomplished more
> than I ever thought I could (considering my upbringing),
> traveled as much as I wanted, always strived to be a good hus-
> band and father, a good employer, a loyal volunteer, a supportive
> friend and good neighbor. I have done so many different things
> during my life that at this point, the thrill is gone.

At 56, I am tired of working, tired of travel, bored with my hobbies and sick of dealing with most people in general. I'm relaxed and laugh easily and have good relationships, but nothing excites me anymore. Honestly, if the Grim Reaper tapped me on the shoulder and said, "Pack your bags; tomorrow's the day," I'd just shrug and ask, "What time?"

. . . I went to a couple of therapists who told me I don't need therapy; I just need to find a new "spark." So what's a person to do? Must I keep wallowing through the days waiting for the end? Am I the only person who feels this way?[9]

The writer (I'll call him Mr. Blah) is by no means the only person who has experienced this kind of torpor. There are millions of Mr. Blahs throughout the world; he may sit beside—or even inside—you. He is quintessentially bored and stuck, disengaged from his work and his life, and like many others, he's been derailed from a path of learning and growth and can't figure out how to get started again.

If this letter crossed your desk as the cover letter for a job application, would you hire Mr. Blah? How would it play as a LinkedIn profile? It may seem obvious that you wouldn't be interested, but it's not as clear-cut as it first appears. Because Mr. Blah, in many ways, fits the mold of a competent employee who stays in their place, does the work they've always done, and rocks no boats. We often manage people to behave this way. To limit their contributions, exhibit no initiative, and not be moved by their work at all. Stay in your lane, Mr. Blah. Employee disengagement numbers are perpetually and depressingly high.

But people who want to grow and develop, who demand that we pay attention to their aspirations, are more challenging to lead. We want our candidates to be overqualified when they onboard and be willing to keep doing what they do forever. Instead, they want more training, additional opportunities, new roles. On second thought, if Mr. Blah made a tiny effort to camouflage his utter lack of interest in doing anything, we might imagine him an ideal employee and hire him on the spot.

But Mr. Blah won't grow your organization. Whether he joins the team with his present mindset, or it's programmed into him by lax management, he's not looking to grow anything. He's not going to posi-tively impact the top line, the bottom line, or any lines in between.

If you want to grow as a leader and grow your business—if you want to drive smart growth—it's the Astrid Tuminezes and Harry Kraemers you want to hire. It is impossible to employ a growth-hungry person who wants to contribute to your organization, help them navigate through the entire growth cycle—to learn, leap, and repeat—and not gain an organizational advantage.

One of the resounding pieces of feedback we receive while teaching these principles across the world is, "All leaders should have this training. This framework provides a common language for talking about talent development. My manager needs this. I need this."

The greatest force on earth is human potential. Nothing is accomplished without it; anything is possible because of it. People are not just the most valuable resources of the organization; they are the organization.

When you as a leader are informed about every person's mindset and expectations around their growth, you can impact their growth. When you not only see them on their S Curve, but *help* them traverse the curve, that's smart growth.

This is the order of operations: grow yourself, grow your people, grow your company.

S Curve Implications for Smart Growth Leaders

The S Curve of Learning gives leaders and their people a shared language for conversations around talent development; healthy longevity at any organization is driven by a worker's perception of their opportunities to grow and develop.

A smart growth leader understands that we all want to make progress, but don't always know how. Sometimes, we don't know where to start or even believe we can start. Once we do start, we can struggle to gain and maintain momentum, and once we have made considerable progress, we may tire of what we've been doing and need to do something new. A smart growth leader gives people the power to make progress by helping them navigate the entire growth cycle—or S Curve of Learning—from the launch point to sweet spot to mastery.

The S Curve Insight Platform, briefly mentioned in the introduction, is a smart growth tool that tracks and monitors individual and collective progress. A fifteen-minute assessment, it indicates how individuals perceive their progress (a powerful undercurrent in every organization), what tools they are employing to maximize their growth, and whether they feel the ecosystem (culture) is helping or hindering their growth. Its results can inform talent development, retention, and workforce and succession planning.[1]

A smart growth leader builds teams with a portfolio of individual S Curves that matches a company's current needs and objectives. Though percentages will vary depending on your industry, size of company, and stage of growth, use the bell-curve distribution as a starting point, with a small percentage of people on launch point and in mastery, and most of your people in the sweet spot at any given time. Track patterns among teams and across departments and business units. If, for example, most people on the sales team are on the launch point, how does this impact launching a new product? What support do team members need to be successful? And how might one of your teams that is in the mastery phase (for example, finance) support them? What support do they need from you? Leverage the strengths and mitigate the weaknesses of each phase of growth.

Just as a biometric device can monitor steps, sleep, concentration, and behavior, it's important to track growth in a role and to understand your individual team members' perceptions of opportunities for, and expectations about, their growth. When you have the data on where people are, you can affect their growth.

In running, coaches sometimes use the rate of perceived exertion (RPE) to coach their athletes. RPE is measured based on how hard a runner feels they are working. In many ways, RPE is a better training tool than external metrics such as a stopwatch. Why? To improve your speed as a runner, you must push yourself beyond a certain threshold, which is unique to you. The way individuals identify where they are on the S Curve is similar. The amount of time spent in a role, feedback received from supervisors, even responses to an assessment may offer insight into an employee's position on their S Curve of Learning, but there is no better indicator than their personal rate of perceived exertion. Is the work too hard, too easy, or just right?

This book is for any individual who wants to demystify the process of personal growth. If you wonder how to start, gain momentum, or why you outgrow things, even things you do very well, this book is for you. Grow yourself.

For any manager or coach looking to decode talent development and succession planning in their organization, this book is for you. Grow your people.

If you are a C-suite executive needing a guide to maximize your organization's human capital in order to maximize your bottom line, I'm talking to you, too.

This is the order of operations: grow yourself to grow your people to grow your company.

PART ONE

LAUNCH POINT

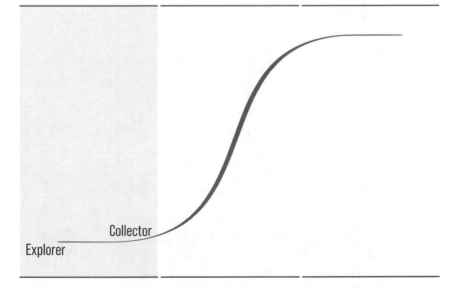

Explorer

Collector

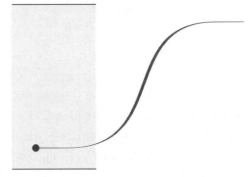

1 Explorer

There is a tide in the affairs of men which, taken at the flood, leads on to fortune. . . . On such a full sea are we now afloat; and we must take the current when it serves, or lose our ventures.[1]

—WILLIAM SHAKESPEARE

Shakespeare sheds light on the decision we face at the outset of a journey, whether literal or metaphorical: Which course do we choose? How do we decide which tide we will take at the flood?

In 2002, Mike Rowe launched his life-changing S Curve—there's no way to sugarcoat this—in a sudden, raging flood of human waste in a sewer beneath San Francisco.[2]

At the time, Rowe was host of *Evening Magazine*, which he described to me in 2020 as a local interest show with a fairly tame format. "I always hosted it from wineries or art openings or restaurants," he said, but "I could go anywhere in the city I wanted to."

Then he got the trajectory-changing call from his mother. Peggy Rowe was calling about Carl Knobel, Rowe's ninety-one-year-old grandfather, a gifted tradesman. Rowe grew up next door to Knobel in Baltimore County, Maryland, and idolized him. "Your grandfather is not going to be around forever," Peggy told her son. "It would be terrific if before he died, he could turn on the television and see you do something that looked like work.'"

Pop, as Rowe called his grandfather, "was the guy who could take your watch apart and put it back together blindfolded." Through much of his childhood, Rowe wanted to be like his grandfather, but frequently he was the bumbling assistant instead. On one such occasion, he messed up a concrete mixture for his grandfather:

> It's like the third thing I got wrong that day. And that was the moment when Pop said, "You're my grandson, I love you. You can do this the rest of your life if you want, but you're beating your head against the wall. What you're really enamored of," he said, "is not the business of building patios or porches or renovation. You're obsessed with the trades, but I don't think you're really obsessed with the construction trades. I think you're in love with the idea of being a jobber; of projects that have beginnings and middles and ends."

Carl Knobel, grandfather and handyman, was talking like a true smart growth leader. When Rowe received the wake-up call from his mother years later, he decided to embrace his jobber mentality. He thought, "Why not host [*Evening Magazine*] from a factory floor, or a construction site, or a sewer?" So, Rowe dialed up the city supervisor and got permission to go underground.

Rowe and his cameraman trailed a veteran sewer inspector named Jean Cruz. They experienced the hazards of the trade firsthand when a lateral line (the pipes from homes that feed into the main sewer) suddenly exploded:

> I'm squatting there in about a foot of indescribable filth, trying to open the show while my cameraman is filming me, and the lateral blows up and hits me in the side of the face, which is pretty funny TV. . . . I was covered by many thousands of thumb-sized roaches. . . . I was assaulted by a rat the size of a loaf of bread. . . . I was baptized in a river of [raw sewage]. At that point, Jean, the sewer inspector—who was busy hammering

out bricks in the main line and replacing them—looked over his shoulder and on camera he said, "When you're done [playing with] the local wildlife, why don't you come over here and give me a hand?"

Another TV host might have been tempted to throw away the tape, burn their clothes, and bathe in bleach. But Rowe saw it differently: "That footage became a short segment on *Evening Magazine* called "Somebody's Gotta Do It," and it got me fired, of course. People are sitting down to watch their beloved *Evening Magazine*. It's dinnertime. They're having their meatloaf and there I am crawling through a river of [waste]. It was the wrong segment for that show, but I loved it."

The station let him keep the footage. Few could have guessed how that decision would give birth to one of the highest-rated reality shows of all time, reaping tens of millions in profits. "I showed the footage to Discovery [Channel]," Rowe said. "[Discovery] changed the name from *Somebody's Gotta Do It* to *Dirty Jobs* and I began a new phase of my career at forty-two."

Uniquely on *Dirty Jobs*, Rowe wasn't a spectator, but an on-air apprentice to pig farmers, roadkill cleaners, hot tar roofers, sewer inspectors, all in service of the question, "What would the world look like if no one did this job?" Perhaps, too, he was asking what the world would look like if no one did the work his grandfather did.

Dirty Jobs premiered in 2005—with Rowe's grandfather watching. It transformed reality television, inspiring dozens of similar shows about Alaskan bush pilots, alligator hunters, and more. Entire cable networks would not look the way they do now without Mike Rowe. More meaningful to him is his ongoing work to shift attitudes in the United States about the workers and farmers that drive the economy, "the essential workers that get dirty on our behalf."

Before the effluvium in the sewer led to three Emmy nominations, Rowe's was a checkered career, with years in the construction industry ("I was a nightmare on the jobsite"), years as an opera singer, even more years as a host on the QVC home shopping channel (he was fired three times), and a multitude of short-term TV gigs. He recalls: "From 1993 until 2001,

I probably had four hundred jobs: working for the History Channel, for Nat Geo, for the Discovery Channel, impersonating a host for anybody who would hire me, infomercials, regular commercials, documentaries, talk shows, pilots."

I'm not recommending that you do four hundred different jobs, but when you are in the Explorer stage, consider Mike Rowe. Until he hit the sweet spot at age forty-two, Rowe made an art form of exploration. He then made exploration the model for his hit reality TV series *Dirty Jobs*.

Explorer Phase Defined

Explorer is the first phase along the S Curve of Learning, and the first phase on the launch point. Your destination is the top of the S, and your pathway is the curve winding to the top of that S. But as an Explorer, you first take time to evaluate the potential of various S Curves and decide where you want to be.

I am here.

Do I want *to be* here?

The Explorer phase is when you consider your destination, even if it seems like the destination chose you, as it sometimes does. It's when you do your homework before committing to a course of action, lest you find yourself at the top of an S Curve you don't care about. Nonexploration, the failure to make conscious informed choices in life, leads to a crisis, whether quarter life, midlife, or three-quarters life. You can allow yourself to be carried on whatever tide is rolling out, but smart growth requires that, whether captain or castaway, you choose your own ship.

What do you want to explore? Have you quietly abandoned the thought that you can still transform your life or learn new things? Or do you have a bucket list of ideas and aspirations you're itching to tackle?

Perhaps you're considering a job or role change, starting or buying a business, getting married, becoming a parent. Maybe you are exploring how to volunteer in your community, how to donate to causes you care about, or how to successfully vacation. You could play the guitar, pick up a sitar, become a tap-dancing TikTok sensation, cook, garden, or cook from your garden. Perhaps you want to learn to invest, find a religion, wallpaper a room, or teach your old dog new tricks. Maybe you want to conquer the territory of self—to develop greater patience and become more focused, resilient, or benevolent. Each is a voyage awaiting a captain.

Exploration is key because it helps us make good decisions despite a mind-boggling array of choices. Most of us do not suffer from a lack of possibilities. Overabundant options can be paralyzing and undermine or discourage action. A few decades ago, grocery stores carried about eight thousand items. Today, they carry forty-seven thousand. Barry Schwartz, professor of social theory at Swarthmore College and author of *The Paradox of Choice*, explains that "an abundance of choice can complicate decision-making," resulting in inaction, or in action postponed by uncertainty and frustration. When "you do make a choice, due to FOBO—fear of better options—you're more likely to be dissatisfied because you think an unchosen item might have been better."[3]

If we struggle to choose laundry detergent, it's no wonder we're mentally exhausted when weighing the complex variables of education, career, and life purpose. Entire industries exist to help companies make multivariable decisions, and yet we, by ourselves, are making these types of decisions every day. Consider the kinds of complex mental analyses and pro-and-con trade-offs that go into purchasing a car, never mind making a truly momentous personal or professional decision. Our prefrontal cortex, the part of the brain that juggles all the options we are considering, doesn't have unlimited processing power to constantly consider how one of the infinite number of new things we could do fits with what we are already doing. It usurps an enormous amount of energy to do this. Tired? Drained? Of course you are.

We're also paralyzed by fear. Exploring a new S Curve of Learning is filled with the threat of uncertainty. Our brain likes novelty, but when there's too much novelty, our limbic system, whose job it is to detect and respond to threats, sounds an alarm. This is the emotional and intuitive part of the brain commonly referred to as the lizard brain. It's warnings generate stress (that would be cortisol) and hyper-alertness (thank you, adrenaline), which causes us to overemphasize the negative. *Why did I decide to explore a new S Curve? There are a hundred things that could go wrong!* Negativity and fear make us even more risk averse. To protect ourselves, we reject the new (this is one reason lizards don't make great CEOs), and we stop growing.

Learning to Go Slow, Faster

Understanding the S Curve process in general reduces anxiety, fear, frustration, and impatience, just as having a map or navigation system eases worries on an unfamiliar trip. It makes it easier to become an Explorer and start the journey.

In the Explorer phase, things will feel *slow*. Possibly uncomfortably so. Here's why:

- *Time seems to expand when you are doing something new.* When we are mostly engaged in familiar tasks, our perception is that time passes quickly. There is little or nothing memorable for our brains to process. When we do something new, the brain is busy recording, making memories of unfamiliar experiences. Our perception is that time has slowed. This partially explains why time seemingly passed more slowly when we were children and everything was novel, but sped up as we aged and the brain compressed a year of routine days into only a handful of memorable moments.[4]

- *Making decisions is taxing.* This part of the curve can be tiring. We are exploring a variety of options to decide what S Curve we want to try, whether it's a new role or a new behavior. There's a lot of analysis involved and the decision-making part of our brains doesn't have unlimited processing capacity. We are simultaneously engaged in all the normal affairs of our daily lives and frequently experience cognitive overload; a traffic jam in our brain.

- *Progress is not discernible.* Our brain is making memories and neural maps, but they aren't yet apparent. I like to use a simple analogy to illustrate this key point; I call it the lily pad of learning. Water lilies begin their lives as a seed or tuber, pushing new roots into the mud beneath the water. From this mucky beginning, a stem grows up through the water toward the sun. These are critical first steps, but they often go unnoticed—under the surface, below detection. *Slow.* Once the stalk reaches the surface, it will sprout its unique circular leaves. Blossoms will appear. Meanwhile, the roots are creeping through the mud, shooting up more stalks, leaves, and flowers in a vast network. The literal, physical expansion of neural networks in our brain is similar. It starts small and slow, almost indiscernible, but as we continue to explore, growth accelerates. Like lily pads on the water, the results of our growth become evident only gradually, and the foundation of that growth in the brain remains concealed, like roots in the mud. But just as we eventually see lily pads on the water, we know the neural networks are developing because the results begin to flower in our lives. When growth is indiscernible, we can feel uncertain and anxious. *Why haven't I figured this out yet?* We may not want to persist. *I thought I wanted to do this, but crikey, this is hard!* We may even want to skip over this phase. *I want to grow! Why do I have to take the time to explore?*[5] As an Explorer, if you feel like you are in the muck, this is normal. Just understanding that the math of the S Curve of Learning dictates that something is meant to feel slow can reduce our feelings of anxiety and impatience. This allows us to actively explore this new S Curve without discouragement, instead of possibly abandoning it when results don't instantly appear.

Marco Trecroce is the chief information officer at Four Seasons—the first CIO ever for this global luxury hospitality company.[6] Before starting there, Trecroce was between jobs for two years. He did some private contracting, worked for a couple of small businesses temporarily, but, he says, "None of them was the right fit." This lengthy exploration period was uncomfortable—slow—but ultimately fruitful. Four Seasons was on the short-list of organizations Trecroce wanted to work for.

His first boss at Four Seasons was the then CFO, John Davison, who instead of pressuring him "to get something done yesterday," as many bosses do, encouraged Trecroce to take his time getting familiar with the organization and its people, thinking through what needed to be done, and creating a plan. For the first six months, Trecroce had space to build relationships and begin to help the various departments and divisions across the enterprise with critical pending IT decisions. Then, a five-year plan was outlined.

One of Trecroce's first big challenges was working with HR to select its next-generation software. When he joined Four Seasons, that decision had been under discussion for over a year. When Trecroce took charge, there was pressure to select a legacy platform. Instead, he chose Workday, a relative newcomer with a different, cloud-based model. Four Seasons was its 178th customer. Trecroce said:

> It was pretty apparent to me this was the way to go. But it took a little while before everyone was comfortable with this decision. The time spent building relationships, understanding needs, and developing trust paid off. If I look back ten years ago, . . . it really transformed the business.

For newcomers to an organization, Trecroce says, "There's a sense of 'I've gotta go fast, I've got to prove myself, I've got to change fast.'" His boss Davison's advice was the opposite: "Take your time, build relationships, and get to know people." Davison, now the CEO of Four Seasons, and a smart growth leader, understood that Trecroce was on the launch point of the CIO curve and gave him time to explore, even if that meant he wasn't seeing results right away. Davison was confident that roots would grow in the mud.

The Explorer's Key Questions

To decide if a stretch of terrain warrants further exploration, here's a seven point template of questions I suggest Explorers ask.

1. Is it Achievable?
Do I believe I can attain it?

The early twentieth-century author Neville Goddard said, "The drama of life is a psychological one and the whole of it is written and produced by your assumptions. Your assumption guides all of your conscious and subconscious movements so inevitably that it actually dictates events."[7]

Wistfully thinking "That would be nice . . ." often signals we don't think a goal is possible and, therefore, won't be. If, instead, we are optimistic, saying, "I am so happy I've achieved this" as if we already have, there is a kernel of belief that it is within reach. In the Explorer stage, you are asking, "Can I see myself doing or being this?"

Often though, there is a gap to bridge. Knowing that our assumptions guide our movement, how do we change our assumptions so "that would be nice" becomes "this is nice"? While it's true that there are unattainable objectives, it is also true that there is a nearly limitless range of things that are possible. They require only that we believe, and act on our belief.

To quote Shakespeare again, "Assume a virtue if you have it not." Four centuries later, we paraphrase, "Fake it 'til you make it."

In 2000, Marcus Whitney moved to Nashville, Tennessee.[8] He was a twenty-four-year-old dropout from the University of Virginia. "I had a one-year-old and another child on the way and was waiting tables six-and-a-half days a week," he told me. His family was living in an efficiency hotel. "I didn't have a lot of leeway or slack in my life."

Whitney did, however, have a starting point, "When I was nine years old, my late Uncle Otis, who was a programmer at IBM, gave me a PC Jr. . . . I learned a programming language (BASIC) and the basic principles of how computers work." As a child, he had envisioned himself as a programmer, so in his mind, a better life was possible.

But it had been fifteen years, and his computer skills were old and rusty. Still, Whitney started studying programming books between serving customers at restaurants. After working twelve-hour shifts, he'd put in another four hours on the computer at home. He applied for hundreds of jobs with little success. It wasn't easy visualizing his goal, but "Having my back against the wall was helpful for removing a lot of extraneous narratives that weren't helping me go where I wanted to go." In his book, *Create and Orchestrate*, he describes how he got through the slowness of the Explorer phase:

> There was more to it than just hard work. My mindset was
> critical. . . . There wasn't a lot of evidence around me that I
> could be successful in making this transition. I had to create a

mindstate supportive of my endeavor. I didn't achieve that mindstate by believing I was becoming a programmer; I achieved that mindstate by believing I already *was* a programmer. This distinction is very important. By believing I already was a programmer, even though it wasn't obvious to others, I bypassed many of the limiting thoughts and doubts about my ability to become a programmer. I never said I was a great or even a good programmer. I just believed I was a programmer. This small tweak of believing we already are what we want to be, rather than becoming it has significant downstream effects.[9]

Marcus Whitney's first paid gig as a programmer was a barter deal. His wife needed a midwife, and the midwife needed a website, so services were exchanged. A year later, in 2001, Whitney got his first paid job as a programmer. In 2003, he was hired as the fifth employee at an email marketing company, later sold to a bigger firm. The founder, his former boss Clint Smith, remembers him well: "Marcus had the ability to play up a level or two—and ended up running all of engineering."

Several startups, two exits, loads of desire, persistence, and twenty years later, Marcus Whitney is the founder of Jumpstart Nova, the first Black health-care venture fund in America. He's the CEO of Health:Further, a health-care strategic advisory firm, and is cofounder and part owner of the Nashville Soccer Club, the major league soccer team in Tennessee.

If we are willing to do the hard work of changing our assumptions, we will begin to believe our goal is attainable.[10] Belief is where an Explorer starts.

2. Is It Easy to Test?

Is there an easy way to test whether I want to be on this particular S Curve of Learning? If I decide to stay on this S Curve, will my initial pace be sustainable?

In 2019, I decided I wanted to be physically stronger. There were many options—I could join an Everest expedition, become a mixed martial arts/ UFC fighter, or run. Setting aside the desirability and believability for a

moment (you probably can't picture me as a UFC fighter, either), how easily could I test if I wanted to jump to one of these physical fitness curves?
Of the three, running is by far the easiest. I tested it by committing to run
five minutes a day for a week, thirty seconds running and thirty seconds
walking.

After a week's exploration, I had enough information to know I wanted
to be on a running S Curve, and I wanted to run at least one 5K. Now I
had to decide on an initial pace for how quickly I would increase the time
and distance I ran each day. Five minutes in week one, ten minutes in week
two, up to fifteen minutes in week three? For me that was too ambitious.
I was looking for sustainable, long-term behavior that would evolve from
conscious and challenging to natural and automatic. I settled on small
increments—a ten-second increase each time I ran. This was a manageable level of effort, to which my brain would say, *I can do that! I did that
yesterday!* even on days when I wanted to just curl up in a chair with one
of our cats.

It took about eighteen months to get to the top of my 5K S Curve, but
because I made it easy enough to start and sustain, I persisted. I now run
three times a week. The behavior has become automatic. I no longer think
of running as something I do. It's part of who I am. I am a runner.[11]

Find simple and easy ways to test new S Curves of Learning. I know
this sounds obvious, but I've found, both with myself and in coaching
others, that once we feel inspired to do something new, we feel compelled
to start really *big*. But when we need to make space on our cluttered mental
and emotional shelves for something *big*, we find there's little room. It's
discouraging. Where do we even start?

Start small. Set your initial expectations and incremental increases so
small, so laughably small, that you deactivate your inner procrastinator.
Each tiny benchmark is its own easy test. Is this S Curve feasible? Can I
sustain this long term? Take baby, baby, *baby* steps.

Top management consultant Darrell Rigby knows early testing is essential to the success of any major innovation. Rigby's fascination with innovation stems from his days at Harvard Business School. Rigby told me he
was something of an oddity there—a "castoff," in his words.[12] He went
straight to business school after university without first paying his dues

on the bottom rung of a company ladder, as many management students do before they matriculate. Landing a crucial summer internship would be a high hurdle for Rigby, and things weren't looking good. He was dismissed as too young and inexperienced. Then he caught a break. "Bain decided to give me a chance," Rigby said, referring to the now prestigious management consultancy, Bain & Company. At the end of the summer, Rigby came away with a full-time offer from Bain. He's now a partner and head of Bain's global innovation and agile practice.

Rigby has spent much of his tenure being an expert Explorer. His process is to constantly ask himself, "How can I make my job at Bain the perfect job?" Step 1: Explore an idea for disrupting the job. Step 2: Test the idea. Step 3: Sell senior executives on the change he has in mind. Bain welcomes innovation, but you need to make your case.

It helps to have leadership that lets you explore and test. For example, fifteen years ago, Rigby saw an opportunity to start an innovation consulting practice. He pitched the idea to Bain's operating committee: "I said, 'Let me try it for six months, and if it doesn't work, I'm happy to find something else. But if it does work, then we've created a new platform that could be good for our clients and good for us.'" They gave him six months to test.

As the leader of Bain's retail practice at the time, Rigby had the idea of helping retailers innovate in order to adapt to the meteoric rise of online sales. Working with some remarkable partners, Rob Markey and Jimmy Allen, who were willing to share their budget allocation and give visible support, Rigby was able to bootstrap the experiment, build credibility and ultimately establish the innovation practice at Bain. As Rigby explored better ways to innovate, he came across agile practices in the technology departments of many retailers.[13] He says, "At first, agile scared me. I didn't like all the jargon. And it was a language I wasn't convinced I wanted to learn, but eventually decided I had to do it." More exploration.

Smart growth leaders willingly try new things and jump to new S Curves of Learning, even when the leap is challenging. Rigby's new S Curve was testing agile methodology. It has since become a core component of nearly every practice area in the Bain system.[14] Forty years and counting, Rigby is still in his dream job.

Influential management thinker and professor at Columbia University Rita McGrath has found that the root cause of failure in new business ventures is viewing untested assumptions as facts. She explained to me that business leaders are susceptible to being caught up in a project emotionally, without taking a hard look at the probable costs and outcomes.[15] "With their eyes on an attractive prize, leaders often underestimate the difficulty of getting there, substituting optimism for data." They explore without testing. Especially with a high-stakes opportunity, it pays to devise a low-commitment test: minimal cost, a short time frame, and a relevant metric before fully committing to the course.

3. Is It Familiar Yet Novel?
Is the S Curve of Learning I'm exploring familiar enough to be navigable, yet novel enough to promote growth?

Explorers should look at S Curve opportunities in terms of both their familiarity and their novelty. You need some of both.

Familiarity helps you relax and feel safer; too much familiarity may mean stasis. The unfamiliar in small doses surprises and delights and can lead us in new directions. Darrell Rigby wasn't familiar with agile methods, but he knew enough to see their relationship to other areas and take on the challenge. In large doses, novelty and uncertainty create anxiety and fear. For me, training for an Everest expedition or becoming a UFC fighter are currently too unfamiliar.

It's important for Explorers to realize there will be *some* discomfort at the start of any worthy S Curve. Psychologists use the term "premature cognitive commitment" to identify the human and animal tendency to cling to familiar assumptions, even when new facts are brought to light. One recent study posits that of the 6,200 or so individual thoughts that we have per day, only a small percentage are new.[16] Cognitively speaking, we rarely explore new routes.

To illustrate the dangers of this, consider that in India, an elephant calf is easily kept in place by being chained to a small stake in the ground. How do you keep a six-thousand-pound adult elephant from taking off? With the same small stake and chain. The elephant is held captive by its premature cognitive commitment: I didn't escape this before. I can't now. Similarly, we may think learning something new is an impossible hurdle, when in fact it's just a token barrier that's easily overcome.

In early 2020, I interviewed Tara Swart, a neuroscientist and former psychiatric doctor, now a senior lecturer at MIT Sloan School of Management, who told me:

> The brain becomes less malleable. The child's easy gift for picking up a language, a subject, or an instrument gives way to the adult's old-dog-new-tricks mindset. From twenty-five to sixty-five, you really need to do things to push yourself through that S Curve. . . . It has to be something that's sufficiently difficult that it makes you sweat mentally, as it were, to actually change your brain.[17]

Academic research suggests there's an optimal ratio of tried-and-true to the new.[18] Brian Uzzi and Benjamin F. Jones, professors at the Kellogg School of Management, analyzed 17.9 million research articles over ten years. They found that academic papers that combined about 85 to 95 percent familiar sources with 5 to 15 percent novel sources were twice as likely to be high-impact papers, as measured by citations. Their conclusion seems to concur with our general human tendency to want *some* new knowledge to build on the firm foundation of what we already know.

It's the same in music: when *Hit Makers* author Derek Thompson studied why songs become popular, he found that "ninety percent of the time people listen to music, they are listening to a song they have already heard."[19] Storytelling follows the same pattern. The hero's journey narrative is so cemented in our cultural consciousness that, from the *Odyssey* to *The Lord of the Rings*, we take it for granted and are shocked when a story deviates from it. That means that only 10 percent of the time we are listening to songs we haven't heard before and watching movies that are truly original. Surprisingly little of what we consume is actually new.

Extrapolating from the research, do you have approximately 85 percent of the know-how you need to succeed on an S Curve you are exploring? Is at least 5 to 15 percent of what you are considering novel enough to stimulate your brain to change and grow?

Entrepreneur Jamie O'Banion was exploring her option to start a business in the cosmetics industry.[20] Much of her exploration told her this was familiar ground. Her father, Dr. Terry James, is a well-known dermatologist who owned a cosmetics lab while O'Banion was still in elementary school.

The science of skin care was dinnertime conversation in her childhood home. As a teenager, she accompanied her father on visits to European and Asian laboratories and manufacturing plants. Later, she was a part-time model and spent time working in marketing and product development at her father's company, where she was exposed to cutting-edge science and scientists, makeup artists, creative directors, and brand professionals.

The industry was familiar. But O'Banion also wanted to start her own business. That was novel, a new frontier of unfamiliar leadership and management skills. She founded BeautyBio, and the mix of familiar and new paid off.

In her 2011 original product launch on Home Shopping Network, her inventory sold out in minutes. A 2016 rollout of a proprietary micro-needling tool netted $4 million in sales in twenty-four hours. Today, BeautyBio is a $100-million-plus business. This may sound like overnight success, but O'Banion's exploration of this S Curve started in elementary school. Her launch point of slow growth lasted two decades. She has successfully coupled beauty product science and continuous innovation while learning essential business skills like putting together a profit-and-loss statement. She's leveraged the familiar and embraced the unfamiliar to achieve impressive, smart personal growth; her business, not coincidentally, has grown smartly too.

Is the ground you will cover sufficiently novel?

4. Does It Fit My Identity?

Is this S Curve of Learning compatible with my identity? Is it compatible with how I see myself and how others see me?

An S Curve worth pursuing will dovetail with who we aspire to be. Exploring areas of ourselves and possibilities that have no apparent connection to who we are right now is exciting. It may even be admirable, but it may also mean we get voted off our current island. People around us, including those we care deeply about, may be heavily invested in who we are now: our family, friends, colleagues, and community. Religious devotion is a prime example. If a particular faith is central to your family's culture or history, even glancing at a map of different belief routes could trigger social backlash.

It's less difficult to take on a new learning curve if it aligns with our current identity. Here, again, balance is necessary. If the new S Curve we're exploring is too aligned with who we already are, the potential for growth may be too low. But if it's too far out of alignment, then the price of reaching for a new identity may be too high. I'm not suggesting we automatically pass over opportunities that are significantly divergent from our current identity. But we do need to explore the cost to our meaningful relationships and our sense of self before we make the leap.

Victor Wooten is a music man. This is his identity. He is a bassist, an original member of Béla Fleck and the Flecktones, and the winner of five Grammy awards. Long before he took the stage at Carnegie Hall, Wooten's first gig was with an eclectic quintet, the aptly named Wooten Brothers Band (his bandmates were his four older brothers). Victor was six years old. "I was born into a band," he says. An older brother started Victor on bass guitar when he was two. "Music is a language," Wooten says. "It's a lifestyle."

Today, Wooten's range of instruments includes bass, cello, upright bass, guitar, keyboard, drums, and percussion instruments. He became a music educator, then a producer, and then the owner of Vix Records, his own indie label. We could imagine Victor Wooten taking on virtually any learning curve in the world of music.

But is it part of Wooten's identity to write a novel? It might be surprising to learn he has—until we meet Wooten's protagonists, three musicians doing battle against an enemy who is trying to destroy all musical sound. Writing a novel was, well, novel, but the creative act and the subject he chose were in harmony with his identity.

However, we'd probably be surprised if we learned that Wooten was exploring computer programming. This doesn't align with how he shows up in the world, to himself or to others. It doesn't mean he couldn't be a computer programmer if he wanted to give that a try. But he would need to be prepared for the emotional, psychological, and social cost that can be attached to such a significant identity shift. Concluding his popular 2019 TEDx talk, Wooten signs off with "My name is Victor Wooten. I'm a musician." A declaration of a positive personal identity.

5. Is the Reward Worth the Cost?
Is what I will gain sufficient to offset the tangible and emotional costs of scaling this new S Curve?

Exploration includes a lot of calculating of cost and benefit. Karen S. Carter started out as an intern at the Dow Chemical Company when just a freshman at Howard University. Carter desperately wanted to finish college, but she knew that her widowed mother could not afford to pay for all four years. Even if it came with the stress of working and studying at the same time, graduation was a dream for which she was willing to pay the price.

She gradually ascended the corporate ladder, but not in a straight line. Early in her career, she was offered a position in human resources. It was neither what she was doing nor what she wanted to do. She declined. The vice president of HR quickly made it clear to her that they weren't asking if she wanted the role—they were telling her it *was* her next role: either grow or go.

Carter wasn't enthusiastic about exploring this opportunity, but Dow was too good to lose. And it was a caring push, not a shove. Carter was in an ecosystem where her potential was recognized. Dow had made a point of periodically offering her plum new roles and growing experiences. Plus, Dow was invested in her growth in the strict financial sense: it had paid for her MBA.

Her reluctant yes to the HR job was yes to a career she couldn't have imagined: Carter is now Dow's chief human resources officer and chief inclusion officer. She describes it as the ultimate stretch assignment. It's challenging, and fulfilling, to oversee people operations at a firm with more than fifty thousand employees. Her creed is that of a smart growth leader: true growth and comfort cannot coexist. She says it's not a question of if but rather *when* we get upended. Disruption is a pay-it-forward principle, so share the tough love: 1) get disrupted; 2) seize the growth opportunity; 3) share it with others. Carter grows herself, grows her people, grows Dow.

Sometimes S Curves aren't totally voluntary. Circumstances, or other people who see potential in us, give us an unexpected push. Preplanned or unforeseen, thrilled or terrified, you'll need to determine whether the reward of being on a specific curve is worth the cost. Even if the reward doesn't initially seem greater than the cost, if you are like Carter, you will find a way to make the numbers add up.

6. Does It Align with My Values?
Is this S Curve of Learning aligned with my core values?

Explorers, ignore this question at your peril.

In 2007, I attended the last day of class for the course, "Building and Sustaining a Successful Enterprise," taught by my mentor, the late Clayton Christensen. In his final minutes with eighty of the world's best and brightest young business students, he could have used his bully pulpit to say many things. He focused on building and sustaining a happy life. He said, "In just a few months you will graduate from Harvard Business School, and embark on what to many, including yourselves, will be prestigious, lucrative, high-profile careers. But if you want to also have happy lives, you need to know the purpose of your life."

That last day of class lecture eventually became a TEDx talk, and a book titled *How Will You Measure Your Life?* in which he shared,

> While many of us might default to measuring our lives by summary statistics, such as number of people presided over, number of awards, or dollars accumulated in a bank, and so on, the only metrics that will truly matter to my life are the individuals whom I have been able to help, one by one, to become better people. When I have my interview with God, our conversation will focus on the individuals whose self-esteem I was able to strengthen, whose faith I was able to reinforce, and whose

discomfort I was able to assuage—a doer of good, regardless of what assignment I had. These are the metrics that matter in measuring my life.[21]

The measurement of our life, in the final analysis, will fall short of what we hoped if the work we are doing, the time we are investing, and the things we are accomplishing don't lead us in the direction of our deepest aspirations and our most deeply held values.

Nearly two centuries ago and just a few short miles from where Christensen lived and worked, Henry David Thoreau said of his time spent at Walden Pond, "I went to the woods because I wished to live deliberately . . . and not, when I came to die, discover that I had not lived . . . I did not wish to live what was not life, [for] living is so dear."

S Curves that become an emotional, spiritual, or physical detriment to us may let us grow, but it won't be smart growth. Not all growth is advantageous. Not all S Curves lead to where we want to go. The S Curves of Learning we explore and ultimately choose to pursue should be true to who we want to be.

That has been the case with Angela Blanchard. For over two decades, Blanchard served as president and CEO of Neighborhood Centers, Inc. (now BakerRipley), the biggest community development nonprofit in Houston, Texas, ranked in the top 1 percent of charitable organizations in the United States.

Much of Blanchard's career has focused on lifting the "lowest-income people, which overwhelmingly included newly arrived immigrants and people of color." She helped them find homes and jobs and obtain US citizenship. Blanchard believes the United States is lucky to receive these high-achieving new taxpayers and wanted to help smooth their transition.

"My focus over the last decade," she told me, "has been on the experience of people displaced by 'war or weather.'"[22] Blanchard is a seasoned executive who has directed budgets approaching $300 million, but she prefers to describe her work with a single word, *service*. Her top value and her true identity are to be a helper in the world to those who have lost everything. Now a senior fellow of international and public affairs at Brown University, Blanchard told me she's "obsessed" with bringing immigrants' stories into the public consciousness. "It's to remind us of our humanity," she said, "because . . . all of us are essentially shipwrecked, trying to figure it out together." Blanchard is living a smart growth life, in part because her expertise and her core values are totally aligned.

Blanchard's case seems easy. She has such a clear sense of her identity and values that the exploration hardly seems difficult. But assessing if an opportunity is aligned with our values is usually easier said than done. We are complex creatures, and our hierarchy of values isn't always straightforward. We have our stated, public-facing values. Mine, for example, are to grow in wisdom (apply knowledge judiciously) and stature (while increasing my height isn't an option, I can accumulate resources to do good), and in favor with God (live according to the standards of a higher power) and humans (treat those around me with dignity).[23]

But we also have hidden or "shadow" values that don't meet the public eye. We live by both. Our stated values can express what we truly want, but often merely express what we think we *ought* to want. For example, we might publicly—even sincerely—express how much we value teamwork, but then conflict arises when our desire for personal credit, a promotion, or leadership status undermines our outward team spirit. Explorers must face the fact that *wanting* to want something is not the same as genuinely wanting it or giving it priority over other, unacknowledged values.

Exploration involves excavating our shadow values. Wanting personal credit, for example, because as a child if you weren't the best, approval was withheld. This dynamic was the seedbed for a shadow value. *Get along with your schoolmates, but make sure you win.* Obscured values are often the default setting that govern our choices, but because they are less socially acceptable and productive than our stated values, we try to keep them hidden. Shadow values may live in the shadow of our consciousness, but they are in relief in our behavior.

Unearthing our shadow values and rooting out the cognitive dissonance caused by holding two conflicting values are essential in exploration. Shadow values emerge to protect us, but left unchecked they will choke our growth, and the growth of those around us. They are like cancer cells and weeds; both grow, but at the expense of healthy ecosystems. It's understandable that we want our less socially acceptable values to stay in the shadows, and yet what we avoid or even run away from is almost always the richest raw material for meaningful growth.

Know what your shadow values are. Understand what aspects of your personality feed them, or perhaps what may have happened early in your life that made these shadow values powerful to you. Then bring them out of the shadows. This both honors the experiences that brought them into existence and loosens their grip.[24] *New York Times* columnist David Brooks expresses the paradoxes of value-oriented growth,

> You have to give to receive. You have to surrender to something outside yourself to gain strength within yourself. You have to conquer your desire to get what you crave. Success leads to the greatest failure, which is pride. Failure leads to the greatest success, which is humility and learning. In order to fulfill yourself, you have to forget yourself. In order to find yourself, you have to lose yourself.[25]

7. Is This My Why?

Do I understand my *why* in life and do I understand *why* I would undertake this new S Curve of Learning? Do these two *whys* intertwine?

In 1980, John Mackey cofounded Whole Foods Market. The future organic food giant began life as a small health food store, SaferWay, in Mackey's hometown of Austin, Texas. By 2000, Whole Foods had grown into the undisputed leader in the healthier foods market, at the same time retail had begun its unstoppable march to the internet. Whole Foods had to keep step. The organization purchased a mail order vitamin business based in Boulder, Colorado, with the intent of making it "the foundation for our own e-commerce outreach," Mackey says. He and his wife moved to Colorado to lay the groundwork for that initiative.

Returning to Austin a year later, Mackey was shocked to discover the senior executive left in charge during Mackey's hiatus wanted him ousted, as did some of his board members. He was the only CEO the company had ever had. Now the board was meeting to decide whether his tenure was over. He recalls, "I was anxious about the meeting because I didn't know what the outcome was going to be. But I got into the stores, and I don't know how else to put it, except I had a spiritual experience. I realized that my higher purpose was to be doing Whole Foods. It wasn't time for me to leave."

That epiphany was a *why* moment, when Mackey realized that Whole Foods was more than a job: it was a purpose. Mackey survived the board meeting. He is still the company's one and only CEO, now forty years on. But the near miss with getting fired changed his perspective. From that moment, Mackey's goal became to be a more loving and conscious leader. A few years after surviving that scare, he announced in a companywide letter that he was cutting his annual salary to $1 and giving his stock portfolio to charity: "I have reached a place in my life at which I no longer want to work for money, but simply for the joy of the work itself and to better answer the call to service that I feel so clearly in my own heart." Mackey later capped Whole Foods executive salaries, set up an emergency fund for employees in need, and started funding nonprofit organizations working to promote animal welfare, sustainable agriculture, and healthier food choices.

Being true to your *why* results in growth. You are conscious of your life's purpose; you're focusing your time and effort in areas that further your purpose. And when you grow yourself, you can grow your people. When Mackey focused on growing himself, his people grew, and so did his company. In 2000 the company's stock traded at $5. In 2017 it was $42, and the retail juggernaut Amazon was preparing to buy Whole Foods for more than $13 billion. John Mackey is the textbook example of a *why* in action, even if he was forced to explore that *why* in a critical, stressful, and compressed moment.

When contemplating a new opportunity for growth, consider what motivates you—the *why* behind what you are doing. As twentieth-century American novelist, poet, essayist, and environmental activist Wendell Berry put it, "The world is full of places. Why is it that I am here?"

Exploring my *why* helped me recognize that I wouldn't stay in the investing business forever. It was a challenging revelation. I was good at picking stocks. I could build a decent financial model. I liked being able to say I was an investor. It made me feel important. This was my identity.

But I didn't find myself thinking about the market when I didn't have to. I was far more excited by investing in people. For example, in 2002, while still an equity analyst, I read Tom Peters's article, "The Brand Called You," published five years earlier. *American Idol* was also beginning to peak in popularity. I decided to start one of our team training meetings by talking about how *American Idol* contestants each had a brand—the diva, the comeback kid, the oddball. I then asked every analyst to think about their own personal brand. Were they a stock picker, an industry expert, a connector? I loved preparing that presentation. I spent every spare minute thinking about these ideas and their implications for my colleagues. And I wasn't being paid to do it—not really.

Five years later, I was investing alongside Clayton Christensen, subconsciously transitioning to what I do now. During a conversation with UN Foundation communications director Chrysula Winegar, she said, "You don't just invest in stocks, you invest in people and their dreams." Bingo. My *why*. This sounds punchy. But it goes to my deeper purpose; when I interact with you, I want to be invested in you—for you to have a greater sense of who you are and who you can be, not just professionally, but personally, as a human being.

If you don't yet know your *why*, Simon Sinek provides a brilliant exercise.[26] Ask the people who know you well why they enjoy being around you, and what their relationship with you does for *them*. If you can get candid, straightforward answers from them, their answers will reveal to you your *why*.

Choosing Your Tide

With the S Curve of Learning, you have a map—a visual representation of where you are in your growth, where you are going and how to get started. You don't yet know if you will stay on this particular S Curve—there are so many possible choices to explore—but you do know that you are choosing to grow.

Whether you are a seasoned Explorer in search of a destination or you already have a clear sense that *this is the S Curve for me*, still take the time to explore. The nineteenth-century English writer Samuel Johnson said,

"The use of traveling is to regulate imagination by reality. Instead of thinking about how things may be, to see them as they are." Exploration, like travel, helps to regulate our dreams and aspirations, making achievement more likely, while protecting us against running off the rails with uninformed enthusiasm.

Thorough exploration of a potential S Curve will help sustain you if your resolve falters along the curve. It gets you to the final and crucial set of Explorer questions: *Why not this S Curve? Why not me? Why not now?*

I make this sound easy; it's not. Smart growth requires dedication, discipline, hard work, a host of things that challenge us and test our patience. We can become frustrated, and we can fail. But the exploration process can help shield us against consequences that are more likely and less desirable when we're not thoughtful and deliberate.

I know this from personal experience. I have enjoyed a measure of serendipity and good fortune in my life and career. I have also undertaken S Curves that seemed cursed, in part because I was not smart in my exploration of them. One of these was a decision to invest in a startup magazine more than a decade ago. It was a friend's dream, and I like to invest in both dreams and friends. Her idea sounded promising to me, and I leaped to the launch point with abandon. In fact, the new magazine got a write-up in the *New York Times* and within a few months had garnered more than a hundred thousand subscribers, a resounding success.

Not so fast. In my enthusiasm to jump on this curve, I had almost entirely failed to perform the due diligence—exploration—that smart growth requires and that I've advocated for in this chapter. Though heavily invested in the project financially, I had little authority. We hadn't articulated a business plan (we'll figure it out as we go) or a process for making tough decisions. And there were many of them, about strategic direction, budget, hiring, cover art, print runs, and more. We had not defined a path to profitability. There was frequent conflict with my partner, and the friendship waned as cash became a concern; it died altogether when the business imploded. Not only did I lose the friend, I lost a crippling amount of money that left my family teetering on the brink of ruin. It took us several years to recover.

Even worse, the episode put a great strain on my marriage. My husband has always been supportive and my most important truth teller, but in this case, I didn't loop him in until after I'd jumped in. It was a huge mistake, because collecting resources—especially human resources—in our ecosystem is critical early preparation on the launch point (more on this in the next chapter). My husband saw some of the warning signs that I blithely overlooked in my enthusiasm and haste. Another friend that I invited to take a key role in the startup told me repeatedly, "You need to better articulate the business plan, especially the decision-making process," but I stubbornly refused to listen to her as well. In the aftermath, it took a while to heal my most important relationship.

The significant and varied lessons I learned from this spectacular fiasco are a testament to what a colossal failure it was. It affected relationships and finances, my sense of self-worth and self-confidence. One of its longer-term results is this book. S Curves are a climb, and climbing has its perils. The goal of exploration is not to eliminate those risks; that would be too ambitious and probably impossible. But thorough exploration can help reduce the risks and optimize opportunities for growth.

Exploration is also crucial because although we can scale multiple S Curves of Learning at the same time, sometimes we must choose between curves.

In 2015, I had to make such a choice. The S Curve of thought leader had emerged as a possibility in 2012 when I published the "Disrupt Yourself" article in *Harvard Business Review* that then turned into a book project. I was preparing for its launch; speaking opportunities and demand for coaching were increasing. A business model was emerging.

At the same time, I was working with Kay Koplovitz and Amy Wildstein, developing a fund to invest in women entrepreneurs. It was another launch point; we were iterating, trying to find the right model to overcome reluctant investment in women-owned businesses. They were savvy partners—I liked working with them.

But it was becoming apparent that I needed to make a choice. Option A: build a business around Personal Disruption. Option B: invest with Koplovitz and Wildstein.

In retrospect, it wasn't that I couldn't do both. But given the intense involvement each required, it was imprudent to be on the launch point of these two particular curves at the same time. I remember a pivotal conversation with executive coach Phil Holberton during a crisp winter morning walk. Holberton told me that I would have to choose. I bristled. I knew he was right, but I didn't want to hear it. For nearly a year, I continued to try to chase both dreams. Finally, my truth-telling husband gently intervened: "You need to make a choice." I listened.

Koplovitz and Wildstein's fund—Springboard Growth Capital—has become successful, investing in, among others, the RealReal and Hint Water. Their work is consistent with my *why*: they are investing in people. In many ways, that partnership was a good fit. I still feel a little pang of sadness. The tide went out. A desirable ship sailed and I wasn't aboard. But none of us can visit every attractive port of call.

Once I decided to dedicate, rather than dilute, my efforts, I started to gain traction on my chosen S Curve. In the coming months, I connected with Amy Humble, who would eventually become the president of Disruption Advisors. Together we are on the S Curve of Learning to invest directly in people. This is the tide I have chosen.

Explorer Takeaways

This phase typically feels **SLOW**

The S Curve of Learning is a powerful tool that helps you find your location in the growth process. It is a map with an X that says, "You Are *Here*." Much as a topographical map tells you what to expect on unfamiliar terrain, the S Curve of Learning demystifies what steps you can take to reach your goals—the pinnacle of your S. The journey is filled with stages that mark your progress. No matter what speed you move through the Explorer stage—it may take two weeks, it may take two years—this chapter will help you in this part of the growth cycle. The more you understand about exploration, the greater your capacity to explore.

The first stage on the S Curve of Learning is exploring. As an Explorer, you are faced with the decision of choosing a new course. Exploring a new opportunity, taking the first steps toward personal and professional growth, isn't just a mental process, it's an emotional journey. Expect both positive feelings (thrill of discovery, excitement from new options) and negative (disorientation, anxiety, discouragement, impatience). You are exploring the unknown and dealing with uncertainty. There will be many questions. You will be learning quickly, but it will feel slow. This is typical. Because it is so uncomfortable, there can be a tendency to not even try or conversely to rush through this part of the growth cycle. But don't rush—this is the time to step back to grow and slow down to speed up. Meanwhile, life is a portfolio of often concurrent S Curves, but too many learning curves at a time can result in nothing completed, nothing mastered. Beware the rip-tide of cumulative stresses. The most successful approaches to new S Curves are characterized by patience and perseverance.

This stage in your smart growth comes with many questions that help you explore. Ask yourself the following questions before committing to a particular S Curve. Continue to ask them throughout your journey, and again when you have completed it in order to detect patterns and make meaning for future endeavors.

The Explorer's Key Questions

- **Is it achievable?** *Is this something I believe I can achieve?*

- **Is it easy to test?** *Can I easily obtain useful feedback to inform my decision and progress?*

- **Is it familiar yet novel?** *Is the S Curve of Learning I'm exploring familiar enough to be navigable, yet novel enough to promote growth? Find the optimal ratio of tried-and-true to new.*

- **Does it fit my identity?** *Is this S Curve of Learning compatible with my identity? Does it align with how I see myself and how others expect me to show up?*

- **Is the reward worth the cost?** *Are the incentives of this new learning curve sufficient to offset the tangible and emotional costs?*

- **Does it align with my values?** *Is this S Curve of Learning harmonious with my core values? To what extent does it compete with my shadow values? Does it lead me in the direction of my deepest aspirations?*

- **Is this my *why*?** *Do I understand my why in life and do I understand why I would undertake this new S Curve of Learning? Do these two whys intertwine?*

Not every puddle will support a lily pad. Water needs to be deep enough—but not *too* deep—with sufficient sunlight and nutrients. Always be in search of a growth-friendly pond, where roots can form, and the shoots of a new S Curve can sprout.

At the launch point of a new S Curve of Learning, take time to explore and evaluate. Map your journey. Find an opportunity with the right fit. Be bold in your questioning. Persevere. Be an Explorer.

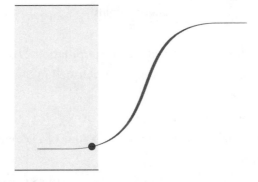

2 Collector

If anyone is going to get in your way, don't let it be you.

—CAROL KAUFFMAN

Entrepreneur Mikaila Ulmer is the founder and CEO of a classic startup success, Me & the Bees Lemonade. It was a $13 million concern at the start of 2020.[1]

In 2009, Ulmer began selling lemonade concocted from her great grandmother's recipe, sweetened with honey sourced from local bees in Austin, Texas. She started out in her front yard and at local business fairs. Soon, a nearby pub wanted to sell her lemonade to its customers. She began bottling on a larger scale. She branched out with new flavors.

Six years in, Ulmer got a break: an appearance on the hit reality show *Shark Tank*. She pitched her business with aplomb and came away with a $60,000 investment from Daymond John. Me & the Bees accelerated from the launch point into the sweet spot. The next year, Ulmer inked an $11 million deal to put her products in fifty-five Whole Foods markets. By 2019, Me & the Bees was available at five hundred stores and selling more than 360,000 bottles a year. Ulmer was developing merchandise as well—hats, T-shirts, branded lip balm, and logo totes. An ardent bee aficionada, she dedicates 10 percent of net proceeds to her Healthy Hive Foundation to support America's now-recovering bee population.[2] Her inspirational book, *Bee Fearless: Dream Like a Kid,* was published in 2020.

At which point Ulmer was fifteen years old.

How could someone too young to have a driver's license accomplish this incredible achievement, earning her a spot as one of *Time* magazine's "Top 30 Most Influential Teens"?

A couple of bee stings had pushed Ulmer onto the S Curve. At age four, Ulmer was stung, twice, by bees in a single week. Recognizing that her trauma could have a lasting effect, her parents encouraged her to study bees instead of fearing them. Ulmer learned about the bees' critical role in our ecosystem, that bees are the pollinators of the food we eat. She learned about bees' twenty-year population decline in the United States.[3] She started a company. Instead of focusing on the pain of the sting, she collected data.

Collecting Data, Learning Lessons

Collector is the second phase along the S Curve of Learning. As an Explorer, we use our mental and emotional capacities to explore our options. Once we have decided on a singular S Curve, we become Collectors. Getting smart about growth in this phase involves collecting both quantitative data found in facts and the qualitative data born of experience. From it, we try to decipher whether we should stick with this S Curve or not.[4]

Progress may not be readily observed. *Slow* is still the essence of this phase. Though impressive, Ulmer's milestones have been gradually achieved. But in the Collector phase we start to get a sense if we're gaining the momentum we need to keep growing. We'll talk more about momentum in later chapters; for now, know that a persistent lack of momentum on an S Curve typically dictates that it's time to move on.

A Growth Perspective

It's normal, even prudent, not to want to invest too much time or other resources on a potential new S Curve, only to discover it isn't really what we want or that it isn't going to work. But it's also true that by the time we are adults, we can be hesitant to even consider S Curves that could be available to us. Our premature cognitive commitments program us to only accept a predetermined range of facts: that we've experienced failure before; that we're likely to experience it again; that we've learned everything we need to, or everything we can. Perception becomes reality, and our growth ends where our pride and trepidation or, in other words, our fear of shame and failure begins.

When I was about eight years old, in one of the spare bedrooms of my grandparents' home, I discovered an upright piano along with my Grandma Charlotte's book *Beginning Piano for Adults*. A kindergarten teacher by day, Grandma Charlotte was learning to play the piano by night. I remember thinking that Grandma was very, very old—possibly in her early sixties! Silly Grandma! I thought. From somewhere in the ether, I had absorbed the notion that learning was only for children: that's why children go to school and take music lessons.

Happily, our understanding of growth has grown up since I was child. Pioneering Stanford psychology professor Carol Dweck was first to use the term "growth mindset." The fact that you're reading this book makes it highly probable that you already have a growth mindset or would like to develop one.

Most of us have a growth mindset—until we don't. Studying cognitive growth in adolescents, Dweck reports that those with a "fixed mindset" believe they are a known quantity.[5] Their intelligence and capability are set, and with that assumption, best practice is simply to avoid looking dumb. But those who exhibit a growth mindset understand that their talents and abilities can be developed through effort, good teaching, and persistence. They don't necessarily think everyone's the same or that anyone can be an Einstein, but they believe everyone can get better if they work at it.

Collect Like a Child

The collection phase is crucial to determine whether the curve we've chosen is the right one for us right now.

That's what four-year-old Ulmer did. After pulling together some basic bee data, she added real-world experience to her hive of information. Her dad helped her in the kitchen and with essential business know-how. Her mom provided marketing assistance (leaders encouraging smart growth, again). More collecting. More supporting data.

Children are S Curve naturals because unfamiliarity is not intimidating to them. From a child's perspective, *everything* is unfamiliar and exists for them to discover. In fact, they can be so unintimidated, they are likely to be impulsive: moving into action too quickly, collecting shiny pennies helter-skelter.

Ulmer's parents helped her honor *slow*. She didn't move out of the Collector phase prematurely, swimming with the sharks before she was ready. A pitch on *Shark Tank* can be brutal; half of *Shark Tank*'s contestants fail to get a deal.[6] The celebrity investors ask hard questions. They are skeptical and tough. So Ulmer first pitched her cautious parents and persuaded them to put aside their desire to protect her from a *Shark Tank* heartbreak. Then they worked together for months to prepare and rehearse Ulmer's pitch for the show, always collecting data.

Caution is not fear. Caution is data collection, gathering evidence that we are on the right curve. Confirming that we've collected what we need so that when we do start to go fast, we don't get stung.

When I asked Ulmer where she is on her S Curve of Learning, I thought she might say she sees herself as having mostly scaled the curve, given the successes she's piled up. But, no, she described herself as still being on the launch point, just ahead of tipping into the honey sweet spot, with still so much to learn about bees and business. About life. "I'm going into my junior year in high school. It's overwhelming. I have to figure out what I have time to do and what I want to do," she said. She's a Collector.

We can learn a lot about collecting data from children. While adults tend to be experience hoarders, hauling the weighty baggage of past failures and even successes, and wary of climbing new curves, a child is more of an experience Collector, wide open with wonder and curiosity. The renowned Italian doctor and educator Maria Montessori is reported to have said, "The child has a different relation to [her] environment from ours . . . the child absorbs it. The things [she] sees are not just remembered; they form part of [her] soul."[7]

When we are Collectors, we gather cautionary and encouraging data about whether we are growing on our curve, whether we enjoy it, and whether we want to keep pursuing it. We collect resources and the ability to utilize them. Like Mikaila Ulmer, we collect emotional and psychological support. And we collect expertise from the people in our environment (see Ecosystem, chapter 7), just as Ulmer collected it from her father's culinary experience, her parents' business coaching, and her great grandmother's heirloom recipe.

We are collecting energy, too: energy to build momentum.

Growth may feel slow, but the promise of "fast" is buzzing in the air.

A young father sent a video to his parents showing their grandson, Ben, riding a bike for the first time. The father captioned it, "First he couldn't, and then he could." He explained that he'd been trying to teach Ben to ride the bike for three frustrating weeks, seemingly without progress. But then, suddenly, Ben took off and rode as though none of the previous failures—even the one just five minutes earlier—had ever happened. For three weeks Ben had listened to his father's instructions, observed his siblings and friends as they rode their bikes, and tried to ride his own. He'd been collecting, thinking, processing, trying to put the pieces together. Growth had been happening out of sight, below detection. On this day, the lily pad of learning had reached the surface of the water, and the leaf unfurled. "All things are difficult before they are easy," said seventeenth-century scholar and churchman Thomas Fuller.

Like children, Collectors are curious and observant, open to learning and suggestions. Questing and questioning.

The Curve That Started with a Caterpillar

Let's look at a second young Collector. To seventeenth-century naturalist Maria Merian, insects were both a fascination and a cause. Merian was born in Frankfurt in 1647. Her father died when she was three. Her mother remarried. Her new stepfather—the still-life painter Jacob Marrel—recognized little Maria's superb gift for art and trained her in his craft.[8]

Merian's favorite art subject was always insects. She began to grow and study her own silkworms when she was thirteen. At a time when less than 15 percent of women in Germany were taught to read, Merian was lucky enough to have access to books on natural history.[9] She read voraciously. A first-rate Collector, Merian collected and studied other insects as well, capturing their intricate detail in her art. In the 1600s, many people in Europe still clung to the ancient Greek notion of "spontaneous genera-tion," believing that insects simply materialized out of litter, dust specks, and mud. Merian knew better. In painstaking detail, she began to piece together the life cycles of her insect specimens.

Still, Merian's bug work was a side hustle while she held down the typi-cal day job of a seventeenth-century woman. She married a painter and raised two daughters; she cooked, cleaned, and sewed. She supplemented her family's income by giving drawing lessons to the daughters of wealthy families in Nuremberg. After a long separation, her marriage ended in divorce in 1692, a disaster for most middle-aged women at the time who would have limited economic opportunities and little chance of remarry-ing. For Merian, it turned out to be fortuitous. Now breadwinners, Merian and her oldest daughter were free to market their own floral paintings; they achieved comfortable financial independence. She expanded her understanding of biology. She mingled with other naturalists. She gained notoriety in the scholarly world as the doyenne of Dutch and English natu-ral science.

At age fifty-two, already beyond the normal life expectancy for the time, Merian obtained permission from the city of Amsterdam to join a scien-tific expedition bound for the colony of Surinam, to study plant and insect life. It's hard to overstate this accomplishment. Merian sold more than two hundred of her paintings to finance the venture. From it came Merian's brilliantly illustrated 1705 book *Metamorphosis insectorum Surinamensium* (*Surinamese Insect Metamorphosis*). It is a scientific landmark. Pioneering botanists such as Carl Linnaeus (1707–1778) would use Merian's work to identify over one hundred different species. Sir David Attenborough called Merian "one of history's most significant contributors to the field of entomology."[10]

Counting the Cost

As with Maria Merian, we may grow intuitively, because of hard work or good fortune, or a combination of both. But if we want to grow faster, we will combine intuition with real-world analysis. What are you observing? What does the data you're collecting tell you?

In the Collector phase, for example, we may discover that an initiative will require more time than we anticipated. This is common. Lasting achievements tend to overrun every aspect of budget. Intrepid Collectors may decide that the opportunity is valuable enough to pursue anyway. Thirteen-year-old Maria Merian wanted to know where butterflies came from. She was willing to invest a lifetime pursuing the curve that started with a caterpillar. Indeed, virtually any plausible S Curve can be scaled if we're willing to devote enough time and effort. Henry David Thoreau wrote, "The cost of a thing is the amount of what I will call life which is required to be given in exchange for it, immediately or in the long run."

When my family and I moved to Virginia, we found blackberry bushes running rampant in the garden. My husband, raised on his parents' pick-your-own berry farm, began tending them: pruning, fertilizing, rehabilitating. He harvested enough fruit to make blackberry jam and dozens of cobblers we shared with friends and family. Surprised by how much he enjoyed the process (as a teenager he couldn't get away from the farm fast enough), my husband considered growing more berries. Could he afford the time? Did he enjoy the work? Would this S Curve yield sufficient growth relative to the effort invested? After counting the cost, he launched into a bigger learning curve. He could have let the blackberries revert to a wild bramble. Instead, he tended them, and also planted strawberries and raspberries. Now we have corn, tomatoes, lettuce, and other greens for the family table and to share with friends. There are wildflowers galore. The S Curve of the garden keeps him growing.

Collect and Curate

As Collectors, we must be keen to spot available resources, and quick to seize and utilize them. This is one of the questions we need to ask ourselves:

Can we (and will we) collect the data and resources we need to accelerate along this S Curve?

Maria Merian collected resources from the scientific community of her day, but also from her discerning stepfather. Jacob Marrel would send her out to the field to, literally, collect both the flowers he painted, and the insects she loved. Her ecosystem encouraged her curiosity and abounded with the skills and resources she utilized in her own work.

At age four, Mikaila Ulmer could not possibly have become a business-woman on her own. But her parents have always helped and encouraged her ("without taking over," Ulmer says). Her plan evolved in her home-town, inspired by the intersection of community "Lemonade Days" and a forward-thinking school business fair in which even kindergartners could participate. Churchgoers bought her lemonade as they came and went from the chapel next to her house. Marye's Gourmet Pizza bridged the gap between paper cups and bottling. Ulmer's little brother was happy to be a taste tester. For Ulmer and Merian, the number one resource to collect was always human.

If you were to compare your growth at this stage to the lily pad's biological system, you might say you are in the pond with plenty of resources available, but not yet in bloom. The speed of the lily pad's proliferation depends on (a) the lily pad's ability to utilize resources, and (b) the room to grow in the pond, or its carrying capacity. Carrying capacity is deter-mined by available resources: oxygen, carbon dioxide, water, nutrients, sunlight, space, and so on.[11] You've explored and are now collecting the data to determine that you can utilize the resources available to you. With ample carrying capacity, the limits of your resources are not yet apparent.

The chief learning and diversity officer at the Kraft Heinz Company, Pamay Bassey implements growth initiatives for Kraft's nearly forty thou-sand humans. She also exemplifies the open, childlike Collector's mind-set. Lifelong learning defines Bassey's career: from Stanford University where she studied artificial intelligence, to her time as faculty at several universities, including the Josh Bersin Academy of global HR develop-ment. Bassey's approach to self-guided learning is elegant: "For over a decade, I have chosen to focus my projects on my interests: the ways people believe, worship, and learn."

Bassey's learning approach stems from her struggle to overcome grief after suffering one of the worst years of her life. Bassey describes 2009 as "total loss." In 2009 her beloved grandmother died, her father lost his long battle with cancer, and as the year ended, Bassey said, "I experienced a betrayal from a loved one. After a year full of loss, I started wondering how I would heal."

Rather than resign herself to despair, Bassey fought back with a yearlong exodus out of the mundane, and into an active collection of spirituality: "My 52 Weeks of Worship Project," she called it. "I visited churches and mosques, synagogues and temples, living rooms and basements. I navigated countless sacred spaces, from the South Side of Chicago to South Africa, from Brazil to Brooklyn." Disruption via worship? Absolutely! Bassey said:

> You might ask: Why spend countless hours in unfamiliar situations, with people I didn't know, experiencing traditions and rituals that I knew nothing about, while sharing my pain and grief with strangers? The answer is that I wanted to believe that goodness still existed in the world. I looked for it everywhere: in the eyes of every person I met, not just at my home church or only in familiar places. My grandmother used to say, "If you are really looking for something, you should look everywhere"—so that's what I did.

Bassey's passion project turned into a book, *My 52 Weeks of Worship: Lessons from a Global, Spiritual, Interfaith Journey*, a companion journal, *Navigating Sacred Spaces*, and a TEDx talk with the same title.[12] Bassey brought a childlike mindset and a wide net to Collecting and found many hospitable and healing ecosystems: "Being open to experimenting, acknowledging that answers to my questions could be found in many different places, was key."

One of our tasks as Collectors is to curate the collection. Out with the outdated, the useless, distracting, and the undermining. We want to rid ourselves of deadweight adult attitudes and reclaim our older, wiser mindset that makes a child a growth machine. Recovering our ability to collect the way a child does, openly and with optimism, isn't automatic, but there are strategies that help. Here are some of them.

Audit Your Adult Self

Your mindset shapes your future, but it's influenced by the ghosts of your past. British neuroscientist Tara Swart, who you met in Explorer (chapter 1), recommends that we get to know those ghosts. Like the guiding spirits in Charles Dickens's *A Christmas Carol*, revisiting ghosts of your past will shed light on the mindset you've developed. She suggests we get acquainted by answering the following qualitative questions:[13]

> *Roles:* What role did I play in my family's social order? How does that role play out now, whether "responsible one," "go-between," "scapegoat," "rebel," or "deputy mother"? How does that role currently serve me?

> *Secrets:* What secrets did my family keep? How did that influence my life growing up? How does that influence me now? What things will I not talk about?

> *Beliefs:* What were the overriding beliefs? Were there unspoken or unquestionable rules?

> *Values:* What were held up as core values in my family? What was more important than anything else? What were the shadow values, those values that I try to keep hidden because they are less socially acceptable but determine what I do?

> *Boundaries:* What was my family's attitude to boundaries: rules, illegal behavior, promise making and breaking?

In your answers you can identify the patterns your mind has developed to make sense of the world and your place in it. Ask those you trust to share with you if there are phrases that you frequently say but without awareness. You will see negative and positive patterns. For example, my daughter pointed out that I frequently say, "I have to do [fill in the blank]." I could be getting ready to go deliver my manuscript to the publisher, a huge privilege. I could be getting ready to go on a vacation, again, a lovely gift, and I will say *I have to*. This may suggest there was a belief in my home that we weren't agentic, that we didn't truly get to choose our course. There are ramifications to holding this belief.

On the positive side, my husband recently observed that when I eat a good meal (especially one that he or my daughter makes), I gush over the food's deliciousness. My mother has always loved to cook; she's written a number of cookbooks. Having grown up in southern Arizona, she was especially good at Mexican food, like chile rellenos and tacos. Food is a love language—a way that I feel and express love.

As you compare the past and present, you'll notice where old ghosts may have crept in, maneuvering your childhood growth mindset toward the more fixed mindset of adulthood. This is essentially an internal audit of your adulthood. Answering those questions will bring subconscious, autopilot behaviors to the surface where you can address them. It helps you understand what you have working both for and against you today, increasing your capacity to access the good and dismiss the bad.

You are a Collector—a *curating* Collector, making space for the new by discarding notions that have exhausted their shelf life or were never useful to begin with. But recognize that this is a process, not an event. And it may be a long and recurring process. Expunging childhood imprinting can be the work of a lifetime. We will likely need to (not *have* to) keep working on it, but it is worth working on.

Pay Attention

Be the person who decides where and how you will invest your most valuable resources: your time and attention. Cultivate childlike wonder but don't give your attention to every passing thing. Science journalist Daniel Goleman writes, "While the link between attention and excellence remains hidden most of the time, it ripples through almost everything we seek to accomplish."[14] Focused attention results in successful collecting.

Collectors can utilize different kinds of attention. Sometimes we zoom out or in to examine a situation either from afar or up close. "Zooming out," says Harvard professor Rosabeth Moss Kanter, "is essential to big-picture decision making, where you map the whole territory before taking action, focusing on general patterns rather than idiosyncratic incidents."[15] The S Curve of Learning is a zoom-out tool. It gives you a map for thinking about growth—a model for the big picture.

Sometimes you will want to zoom in. You may not have an overall picture of how you want to grow, but, as Kanter says, "you understand an industry, have a wide personal network, and even keen intuition. This often occurs in relationship-intensive settings." You've got a lead: someone knows about an open position; someone in your network suggests a class to take, a workshop you need to attend. Zoomed-in data collecting adds detail to your understanding.

One of the most powerful ways of both curating and collecting details—zooming in—is to create what Tara Swart calls an action board, a collection of images of something you aspire to. Some people call it a dream or vision board. She and I both prefer the term "action board." An action board helps us achieve the childlike growth mindset. Here's how: First, selecting images that are meaningful to you is a curation process. You are saying, "This is what I want. This is an S Curve I want to be on." Second, because images bypass our conscious thought and directly access our subconscious, our brain doesn't filter them out or easily dismiss them. Images are emotive and symbolic; they create much more impact than a to-do list. Third, an action board harnesses our selective attention. Our brains are continually selecting (and deselecting) information. We are constantly blocking huge amounts of information. There may be pieces of information, or people we meet, that could help us grow but we are currently deselecting them. Much as when you decide to plant a garden you start to see opportunities to plant everywhere, an action board will prime your brain to collect more of what you need to make your garden grow.

In 2004, I was still working on Wall Street, commuting back and forth to Manhattan from a Boston suburb, and traveling internationally. I loved it, but I was spending very little time at home. During that time, professional photographer and dear friend LaNola Kathleen Stone came to our home and spent an entire day photographing our family. She then curated the photos into a beautiful book: *A Day in the Life of the Johnsons*. I cherished those images of myself at home with my children. Even today, I keep a couple of snapshots in the bookcase in my office. The thirteenth-century

German philosopher Meister Eckhart said, "When the soul wishes to experience something, she throws an image of the experience out before her and enters into her own image." I don't think it's a coincidence that soon after the photo shoot I made a significant career shift that allowed me to spend more time at home. The book of photos was, unwittingly, an action board.

Your action board won't look like mine. It needn't be large or arranged on aesthetic principles. It can cover an entire wall or be small enough to fit in a private space, like on your phone. My current action board is the 1 Second Everyday video diary, an app on my phone that combines a series of one second moments into a film, where I curate images of what I care about. If you aren't ready to do a whole action board, then think of one thing you want and save an image of it, either on your phone or printed out. Look at it every day for a week. If it feels a little vulnerable to pull up the image, then you've got the right one. This isn't Pinterest; it's serious science. Collecting images reinforces your commitment to an S Curve, and an action board primes your brain to collect the resources you'll need to proceed.

Collect Feedback

Our brains like to block feedback. When our standard operating procedure gets challenged, it can feel like an all-out war on our identity. In his book *On Combat*, Dave Grossman explains that a universal phobia (an irrational, overwhelming, uncontrollable fear) is interpersonal human aggression.[16] "When the causal factor of a stressor is human, the degree of trauma is amplified as compared with stress resulting from random events such as traffic accidents." So, in addition to being addicted to being right (our brain floods with adrenaline and dopamine when we're right—more on that in Accelerator, the next chapter), if someone gives us negative feedback, it can be emotionally traumatic. I think this is one of the reasons we like our biometric devices. We get feedback that's personalized, but not *personal*. It feels emotionally safe.

The price of a new, better self is the old self. We pay for it with our openness to feedback. Feedback gets us to focus our attention on things we don't see or may not want to see. Children, again, tend to be naturally good at this; as long as they aren't ignored or shut down, they're willing to be wrong, to make mistakes, to be untaught, to be unashamed. Though they may resist some correction and discipline, children naturally pursue how and why things work the way they work, and how they might work better—a personal set of best practices.

Scott Pulsipher was able to collect feedback to great benefit. He is president of Western Governors University (WGU), an all-online educational institution and the largest university in the United States. Previously he led the building of an e-commerce startup business within a business at Amazon.

It was the day of his second annual review in front of Jeff Bezos and the senior team. The year before, early in Pulsipher's tenure, he'd been sent back to his office to refine his strategic plan and progress report. He expected the same thing would happen this time. As Pulsipher sat and watched, Bezos and his team would read his report for an hour. Then the conversation would start. Bezos told Pulsipher that his was one of the three worst-performing units within Amazon: "Seven out of ten customers hated our product."[17] Pulsipher thought he might lose his job at this meeting.

Here are a few of the things he told me about anticipating this ordeal:

"I had to somewhat emotionally separate from the whole thing."

"Whatever Jeff feels or says about our business, it doesn't change who I am. . . . I had to recognize that it didn't diminish my self-worth."

"I had to mentally go through the process of 'He could fire me on the spot, and I will still be OK.'"

Pulsipher reports the result of this reflection was that by the time the actual review began, "My anxiety level came down and I could sit in the meeting with my back straight, confident, well-reasoned, while still owning the problem."

There are some important truths about receiving feedback here. We need to become dispassionate about it; it's not a judgment of our human value. We need to know that failures are not terminal. We need to understand that it can be good for us, game-changing even, as this review turned out to be for Pulsipher.

Pulsipher wasn't fired; he wasn't sent back to his desk to revise. In fact, Bezos gave his stamp of approval to Pulsipher's plan and his strategy and told him to go execute.

In the following year, he executed a turnaround, reporting on his progress during regular meetings with Bezos: "Once a quarter, I got to have two hours of time with the most senior leaders at Amazon." More support, more feedback, which I believe still serve him today as he has grown WGU to serve 130,000 full-time students, most from underserved demographics, with extremely high completion rates.

We can cultivate a pipeline of constructive feedback by going back to those who provide it and thanking them for their input and interest in us. Remember, the intent of feedback is usually the message "you matter to me." Even if it feels confrontational, feedback often signals that *I am invested in you. I want you to grow.* Once we receive feedback, circling back and sharing what we did with it helps others feel valued and motivates them to remain invested in us. It's like friends who, knowing we collect seashells, watch for shells to share with us.

One thing to note. When we think of difficulty with feedback, we are usually thinking about negative feedback, but we can also be reluctant to receive positive feedback. Compliments can make us bumble awkwardly, rather than simply saying thank you. I try to write down the positive feedback I collect so that I don't forget it. Playing to our strengths helps us climb an S Curve faster. Sometimes those strengths are invisible to us, so we are fortunate when a benefactor points them out. Collect that, too.[18]

To confirm you are on the right curve, become an expert Collector of feedback. Once you recover your childlike unabashedness (and reassure people you won't retaliate), the floodgates of feedback will open.

Here's a detailed example.

Recently, the editors at *Harvard Business Review* were kind enough to audit our *Disrupt Yourself* podcast. They identified technical "trouble spots" and other pieces we might change or improve. Critiques ranged from needing to upgrade the sound quality, to improving my interviewing technique, to clarifying the theme of the podcast.

Collecting their feedback was only the first step. After that, I needed to act. On the sound quality, I don't have or want the know-how. This is not an S Curve I care to climb. So, I collected resources that I can leverage, in the form of people who do, like sound engineers who have chosen audio engineering as their S Curve.

The job of clarifying the overall theme and becoming a more effective interviewer, however, was something I needed to do. I started collecting examples of podcasts featuring great storytelling and pitch-perfect interviewing. I hired a consultant to help me apply their techniques in my own podcast. I got voice coaching. I asked my sound engineers for feedback. They were reluctant at first, but I was relentless. Then came the hardest and most important part: I started listening to my earlier interviews. I confess that in the early days of my *Disrupt Yourself* podcast, there were many episodes that I never listened to. When I was finally willing to face myself and listen, to determine where I was on my interviewing S Curve, to collect data, I grew my competence, I grew my audience. And from audience feedback, I knew I had helped others grow too.

Collectors Gotta Collect

I interviewed Sandy Stelling in 2020 (after receiving the feedback from HBR).[19] Stelling is a twenty-two-year veteran at Alaska Airlines, where she is vice president of strategy, analytics, and transformation. It's a fitting title for an executive who has transformed her own career many times, a career built on masterful collecting. Collectors, after all, gotta collect.

Her high school dream was to study at the Air Force Academy—until a less-than-perfect eye exam shot that down. But Stelling was resilient. Physics and calculus being her fortes, Stelling graduated from college and joined Boeing as a systems test engineer, working on the oily bits of airplanes: landing gear, jet turbines, the mysterious gadgetry you glimpse in the cockpit when you're boarding. Systems tech was a good start, but not a final career destination.

The job she wanted at Alaska Airlines required intense data and resource collecting on a time-constrained launch point. Alaska Airlines was in the market for an IT project manager and tasked Stelling with ensuring computer tech could support new flights from Seattle to Tucson and DC. When she started, she asked where the checklist was. There wasn't one. Her approach was, "So let's build one. Let's find a process to get us through this."

Airports have a lot of moving parts—pilots, aircraft, technicians, customer service agents—and moving parts were quickly becoming Stelling's specialty: "I just kept storing all the information I was gathering to create this mosaic of the airline." After her three-year stint as a project manager and five years in IT, Stelling switched gears to airport services ("not a natural progression"), which involved the wild card of dealing with customers.

After five years there, collecting people skills, Stelling moved to aircraft maintenance. A surprised vice president with thirty years' tenure asked her why. Nobody wants to move to maintenance. She told him, "I was asked to take the job. . . . I like to be of service. . . . There's a first time for everything."

Career transformation number five: customer research and development. Stelling wrote her own job description and moved in ("I think you have a gap and I can fill it"). Three years later, Alaska acquired Virgin America. Versatility and data-collection prowess were essential to integrating the companies. They wanted her to work on the merger.

When she asked what they wanted her to do there, they said, "You'll figure it out."

Now vice president of strategy, analytics, and transformation, Stelling has played a key role in the airline's response to the Covid-19 crisis, the most brutal crisis the industry has ever faced. The long-term strategy they'd worked so hard to develop had to be transformed under duress.

But Stelling knew Alaska Airlines from tarmac to C-suite. The data and experience she'd collected over two decades and across her varied roles made her a central figure in coordinating Alaska's response to the pandemic. She said to the executive team, "I see where I plug in here," and she plugged in. Stelling's experience embodies the Collector mindset: I can figure it out, I can find a way.

The Collector's Notebook

It's a good idea to keep a log of the metrics we set for ourselves. A daily record of our reaction to people and events in our life can shed light on where we are still giving in to self-sabotage, and where we are achieving the childlike growth mindset.

For example, I like to sort through the data of my day for the best moment, and then ask myself how I was creating in that moment. When I shift to the worst moment, it commonly involves some type of competition. My supposed adversary could be another person, or it could be myself: the image of who I think I am supposed to be or what I am supposed to get done. In competitive scenarios, the internal chatter tends to be negative.

Best moment	Worst moment
How was I creating?	With whom or what was I competing?
How did I talk to myself?	What was my self-talk?

What I have discovered is that a day's worst moment often hinges on something that I didn't do or didn't try to do because I thought I couldn't. But this audit makes me aware of that quirk. Being aware is always a prelude to change.

By contrast, in my best moments I was usually fully immersed in what I was doing; my internal dialogue was kind and encouraging. I was feeling confident. In real time, I was becoming more of the me I want to be. (We'll talk more about this in Metamorph, chapter 4.)

Collectors keep records of the data from their explorations, lest information is lost as quickly as it's discovered. I advocate for a journal. Recording data prevents achievable goals from being forgotten and progress from being lost in the shuffle of daily routine. When progress is measured and reported the rate of improvement accelerates, even if we are only reporting to ourselves in a private log. Former GE executive and journaling virtuoso Bob Cancalosi taught me to review my journal every thirty days.

As I review my journal, themes and patterns emerge. And, more importantly, I can detect the subtle growth I've achieved and feel the psychological boost of accomplishment. Regarding her landmark diary, Anne Frank wrote, "I can shake off everything as I write; my sorrows disappear, my courage is reborn." In the hellish ecosystem of the Nazi-occupied Netherlands, Anne Frank collected courage from her diary. We can collect courage too, when we recognize progress along the slow base of our S Curve.

Use Your Words

Being a Collector means seeing yourself as a Collector: a person who has already taken on the identity associated with an S Curve that is underway. As an Explorer, you assessed your identity. You determined who you were at the launch point, and who you wanted to be going forward. Now it's time to acknowledge your new identity, no matter how nascent.

A simple grammar exercise will help you do this. Imagine your S Curve goal is finishing a marathon. Instead of saying "I run" (verb), start saying "I am a runner" (noun). Using a noun rather than a verb represents "an opportunity to become a certain kind of person," says Stanford University psychology professor Gregory M. Walton. This subtle switch is what Walton calls a psychologically precise intervention. "These interventions are much like everyday experiences," he wrote in 2014. "They aim, simply, to alter a specific way in which people think or feel in the normal course of their lives, to help them flourish."[20] Walton shows, for example, that a group of individuals who describe themselves with the statement, "I am a voter," had an increase of 11 percentage points in their voter turnout compared to individuals in a group that self-described with the statement "I vote."

Saying "I am a writer" makes it more likely that the book will get finished than saying "I write." As a Christian, I find it powerful that Jesus repeatedly proclaims himself with "I am" statements: "I am the Good Shepherd," "I am the Bread of Life," "I am the Living Water." To grow smarter and faster, we need to use "I am" statements to help us self-actualize. You're a pianist, you're a runner, you're a Collector.

That "I am" moment of self-actualization is one of the markers of moving past the Explorer phase and into the Collector phase. Marcus Whitney, the self-taught computer programmer you met in the Explorer chapter, didn't explore for long. He had the desire for economic mobility. He determined programming could get him there. His exploration—though brief—was long enough to know he wanted to be on this S Curve. This allowed Whitney to move into the Collector phase where he could begin to study, to practice, and to collect relationships with people from whom he could learn. "I was very, very fortunate," he said, "to have an uncle who was a programmer." He could see him, so he could be him. "And who gave me a computer so I could learn." Whitney collected proof points that he could be on the computer programmer S Curve. He said, "I am a programmer," and so he was.

A Flying Leap

As we collect data, a new idea or behavior is on probation. There will be some things we try more than once, but then discontinue. Even the things we ultimately decide not to pursue can contribute to our growth.

Our dreams, like those of Eric Schurenberg, can change over time. In the late 1970s, Schurenberg would have been surprised to learn that he would become head of the publishing powerhouse Mansueto Ventures, home to *Inc.* and *Fast Company* magazines. An outsider may see Schurenberg's career as a textbook example of the corporate climb: managing editor at *Money* magazine, then editor in chief at CBS MoneyWatch, later, president and editor in chief at *Inc.* An upward trajectory. But in 1978, he hardly knew what business journalism was. Back then, Schurenberg was an actor.

The future *Inc.* CEO, Schurenberg, is listed in an old *New York Times* theater review as one of the fictional bar goers in *Sing Melancholy Baby*, 18th Street Playhouse, New York City. Theater wasn't a bad S Curve for Schurenberg. He graduated magna cum laude from the theater arts program at Brown University and over six years he steadily rose in showbiz. But "it wasn't what I wanted," Schurenberg told me when I interviewed him. So back he went to the launch point to explore a new curve.

Publishing was familiar to him. Schurenberg says about his theater arts degree, "There was a little bit of acting going on, but mainly it meant I read a lot of plays. It was a literary course as much as anything else." He says, "All through school, people had told me I was a pretty good writer."[21]

He did some investigative collecting—evidently rookie writers were getting jobs out of a "Publishing Procedures" course at Radcliffe College. Schurenberg enrolled. He landed his first publishing job: a rookie writer at Time-Life Books.

Being a journalist may seem like a far cry from being an actor. It's often only in the aggregate that a Collector's disparate abilities start to demonstrate unifying themes. As his star began to rise in the publishing world, Schurenberg found himself talking to the biggest actors on the global business stage. "Suddenly, I had gone from being at this arm's-length remove from the people who make the economy go, to talking to them directly and . . . meeting them face-to-face." After he became editor of *Inc.*, Schurenberg was at a financial conference that happened to be just down the street from the old theater where he had once played onstage.

> I took a quick break from the rubber chicken dinner and walked down to the theater. . . . I was absolutely gripped by laughter. It was a kind of philosophical laughter. "How on Earth did I get from there, George Street theater, to this financial conference?" It seems so improbable.

But there was yet another S Curve waiting in the wings, one for which Schurenberg had been collecting data since he was a child. He dreamed of becoming an airplane pilot.

"My father was a guy who wanted to be a flyer his whole life . . . but responsibilities made him rule that out," he told me. Though he never became a pilot himself, Schurenberg's father was an aviation aficionado to such an extent that he built full-scale, working models of biplanes at their home, a couple of which are now in museums. "I was such a geek as a kid," Schurenberg shares, "and so interested in aviation that I won an award from the Greater Cincinnati Library for my collection of books about World War One aviation, some of which are autographed by the aces who were profiled in the books."

As time passed, this childhood dream of a flying S Curve sputtered. Schurenberg said, "[It looked] like I might be going on the same path as my dad: just being an admirer from afar." When I asked how his dream finally took flight, Schurenberg taught me a key Collector principle: "I broke the goal down into achievable parts. The hard part was getting started, but once I did, there was a regimen, like military flight training with a schedule and milestones and dates attached."

Eric Schurenberg received his pilot's license in 2020. The S Curve was steep. The personal cost was considerable. But Schurenberg's drive was considerable, too. One of the factors that brought his dream to life was the relationship between his goal and his core values. He had struggled with this decision. "How can learning to fly be important if it doesn't aid the greater good?" he wondered. Contributing to society is a core value for Schurenberg. But, he says, "I also valued being true to myself. And I felt that my life would be incomplete if I did not master this skill." He concludes, "Now that I have this skill, I can bend it to social good."

I would add that if we don't do something we know we need to do, we are withering, not growing, and very little social good ever comes of that.

Some S Curves are puddle jumpers: some you will hop on, and some you will hop off. This is not failure; this is exploring and collecting. You only keep some model airplanes. You keep some butterflies. But even those S Curves that we ultimately discard can contribute to our growth. No learning is ever wasted.

Like Schurenberg, Canadian-born attorney Marie-Louise Skafte had been collecting data on her dream of flying a plane since childhood, inspired by her father who was a former member of the Royal Danish Air Force and then a commercial airline pilot. "I would sit in the cockpit with my dad and observe," Skafte says. "My love of flying even caused me to apply for a part-time flight attendant's job in law school, which I kept in my early years as a practicing attorney."[22]

The odds were against Skafte ever earning her wings. But she told me, "It was always a nagging feeling that I needed to pursue it." As a biracial woman, Skafte notes that women represent roughly 6 percent of pilots, and Black women less than 1 percent. "I've been the 'first' and the 'only' in many aspects of my life," Skafte said. Told "Blacks don't swim" by her regional swimming coach, Skafte switched swim clubs and went on to become the only Black woman in Canada competing at the national and international levels, ditto at Cornell University. Skafte served as vice president and general counsel of marine shipping container industry leader Cronos Limited in a time when less than 5 percent of transportation management or C-suite officers were women, and even fewer were minorities. While others scare up data suggesting she can't, Skafte collects and stockpiles evidence that she can.

Like Schurenberg, Skafte broke down the piloting S Curve to make it achievable—collecting one data point, then another: "I started with 'discovery' flights at a few different flight schools to find the right fit. Because of my limited availability and extensive travel for work, I needed a school and an instructor who understood that I was one of the few who weren't doing this 'the fastest way possible.'" It took her four years to obtain a multi-engine commercial pilot's license. The costs in time, stress, and money were high.

Eric Schurenberg and Marie-Louise Skafte are you and me. We each have dreams we've carried, dreams others may have told us are implausible, impractical. Maybe we've told ourselves that, too. We can't go back to our childhoods, but as their experiences demonstrate, we can choose to go back to the childlike curiosity and hope that first conceived those dreams.

Sometimes it's hard to get started. The slow pace at the launch point of a new S Curve can defy us. But if we take time to explore, we will find the right fit. By collecting quantitative and qualitative data and resources—and curating to eliminate the deadweight—we prepare to tip into the sweet spot of momentum. We record the answers to our questions, and we track the progress we make, however slight and slow it may seem. It is still possible to course correct if our collecting reveals compelling reasons to do so. But our goal is to proceed with suitable caution and the childlike mindset that keeps us from getting in our own way.

And then, suddenly, we'll throttle forward. Taxiing will give way to acceleration. The end of the runway approaches. Excitement and jitters notwithstanding, we are ready to fly up this learning curve. Slow, fast, slow—that's how we grow. Fast has arrived.

Prepare for the thrill.

Collector Takeaways

This phase typically feels **SLOW**

The second stage on the S Curve of Learning is collecting. As an Explorer, you used your mental and emotional capacity to explore many options. Now that you have decided a particular S Curve merits further exploration, you are a Collector. You collect the quantitative data of facts and the qualitative data of experience. You are collecting data that supports sticking (or not) with this S Curve. Progress is happening, but it can be hard to spot. *Slow* is the essence of this phase.

This part of the launch phase involves recovering your brain's ability to collect the way a child does: openly, with optimism. Yet it can include such a large volume of new information to process, and important decisions to make, that your brain can overload. The excitement associated with novelty can quickly give way to stress and alarm. The stress-linked brain hormones adrenaline and cortisol make the challenge of sorting new information and making decisions even harder. The Collector phase makes you confront how this new S Curve may impact your identity. Growing in this area may clash with the way others see you, or it may not fit in with the way you see yourself. Stress can result when you feel uprooted from your old self, even if you're dissatisfied with who you are.

As a Collector, you identify and collect the resources you need. Then you make room for those resources by eliminating ghosts of self-doubt. You furnish your mind with the growth mindset of childhood. Three tips for being a world-class Collector are to:

1. Audit your adult self; get reacquainted with your childlike self.

2. Pay attention and cultivate childlike wonder consistently.

3. Become a world-class Collector of feedback.

When you approach new opportunities with a childlike mindset and collect data without reservation, you can evaluate whether growth, however slow, is leading to momentum. Does the data you're collecting support staying on this path, or does it suggest you move on to another? Some S Curves are puddle jumpers: you hop on, you hop off. This is not failure. This is collecting.

Launch Point Summary for Smart Growth Leaders

As the lily pad grows, so grows your company. Leaders who commit to seeking smart growth by exploring potential and possibilities with their people will inspire and accelerate organizational growth. Just as the roots of one lily, no matter how small they start, can ultimately fill a multi-acre pond, so can one person's growth revolutionize an industry, employ thousands, change societal attitudes, and uplift our world. Group progress hinges on this truth: the fundamental unit of growth in any organization is the individual.

The launch point of the S Curve feels *slow*. It's not that growth isn't happening; it's that growth may not yet be apparent. There is an amalgam of emotions—excitement, terror, discouragement, impatience. Stress levels are typically high with so much to process; making decisions is cognitively taxing. Confidence toggles between under- and overconfidence (hence the impatience). Questions about identity emerge—*Who am I if I am not who I was?*

The hallmarks of the launch point are outlined in the following Goldilocks Table. Right now, the chair is not too small and it's not just right. It's too big, and it's supposed to be. Once you know what it looks and feels like to be at the launch point, you can create an ecosystem where your people can successfully move through this phase of the growth cycle.

GOLDILOCKS TABLE

Plotting the Emotional Journey of Growth

Dimensions	Launch Point: Slow
Confidence	The feeling of confidence is seldom aligned to reality at the launch. Some personalities will feel no confidence in this new area and fight imposter syndrome and insecurities that drain their energy. Other personalities will feel more confident than their limited experience warrants, leading to costly and avoidable mistakes.
Identity	Difficult and deep questions emerge: • I'm not good at this. Do I have value? • Is doing something like this aligned with who I am . . . or even want to be?
Familiarity	Much about this area is brand new, like exploring a new country. Past experience in other areas can provide valuable orientation but should be treated cautiously so you don't miss the important details and differences.
Mental state	Some personalities find this stressful, feeling overwhelmed by the volume of new information to process and things to learn. Other personalities find all the new stimuli exhilarating. Both need to keep these tendencies from pulling them off the path of deliberate growth.
Value proposition	Considerable untapped potential waits on the other side of the investment. Uncertainties remain, but the reward seems worth it.
Successful mindset	Success at this stage flows from leaning into the challenge: saying yes and experimenting with new approaches, ways of being, and relationships.
Support network	A supportive network may be available, but you generally don't know who those people are or how to access them . . . and even if you did, you're not sure you'd want to because you don't want to look needy.
Decision approach	The tendency for most is to directly follow the procedure and guidance of authority figures.
Knowledge base	You are starting to learn important facts and the needed language . . . but not enough to be efficient or effective. You can think you know more than you do because you don't know what you don't know.
Energy and output	For most, this new challenge takes more energy than expected, and the progress is slower than expected.

Grow Your People: Managing People at the Launch Point

What people on the launch point need from you, their manager, is support. What we are seeing in data is that individuals on the launch point are very aware that their work output is lower than their colleagues and that their capacity (for example, current skills and abilities) to complete their work is lower than that of their colleagues.

At the same time, a majority of the launch pointers are actively working to improve their situation. Make sure they have the tools, resources, and training they need to do their job; ensure they feel that what they are contributing is of value (which includes their inexperience and the "Why are we doing it this way?" question), that missteps are openly discussed (there will be many because the people on the launch point are exploring), and that there are learning opportunities. Collective output is essential but reinforce that their individual growth is a priority to you. (For more on how to create an environment where growth is possible, see Ecosystem, chapter 7.)

Below is a summary table of how to manage people at the launch point based on both the career stage of the individual and the type of organization in which they work.

HOW TO MANAGE PEOPLE AT THE LAUNCH POINT
Leading at Launch Theme: SUPPORT

	TYPE OF ORGANIZATION		
	Young and/or growing	**Advancing and/or midstage**	**Historic and/or complex**
Early career	Set expectations that there will be minimal structure and process, and what process there is will change because the company itself is in the exploration phase. Questions are welcome as people explore, but in order to excel, drive and personal initiative are imperative. Bring on people who are nimble: people who can do what needs to be done, whether showing up for a sales call or scheduling the call for someone else.	For an organization in the sweet spot, it is easy to stop focusing on what is working well as you attend to what isn't. You are no longer so small that collegiality is enough for people to acclimate. Ensure that you have a thoughtful structure in place for onboarding. Some companies do a great job for the first 45–90 days, forgetting that it takes up to six months for someone to understand their role well enough to move into the sweet spot.	Established companies (i.e., operationally in the mastery phase) tend to have strong systems in place to support individuals on the launch point of the curve. Know, however, that your highly driven launch point individuals and teams need to be able to "color outside the lines" at times. The same process and structure that is helping them grow may also constrain them. Support them in their questioning. Reward them for doing exploratory work.

(continued)

	TYPE OF ORGANIZATION		
	Young and/or growing	**Advancing and/or midstage**	**Historic and/or complex**
Midcareer	Help your midcareer employees understand that their skill set is highly valued. You are relying on expertise and intuition born of experience to guide the company through an exploratory phase. Create ample opportunities to hear from this cohort.	Midcareer launch pointers can be the collective engine that helps your organization accelerate into the sweet spot. Ensure people are quickly activated with the resources they need. Consider pairing them with teams that identify as experts and are in the mastery phase.	Midcareer professionals are accustomed to tapping into the tools and skills to be successful. They are on the launch point because they want a challenge. Too much structure and complexity can be demotivating.
Expert career	While an expert showing up on the launch point might be a surprise, don't mistake their technical mastery for an understanding of your culture, your business, or your leadership style. Emphasize partnership, but don't skip the introduction. This support will help you best leverage their talents.	When you attract an expert-level career jumper or move a master into a completely different role, it is typically because they are in search of a new challenge. Do you understand what that is? Are you tracking your ability to deliver on the something different? Experts willing to do the exploratory work involved on the launch point can be rare. Satisfy their hunger for self-disruption. Track the number of masters moving to the launch point as a way to gauge your ability to retain top talent.	This exhilarating jump to launch point gives experts an opportunity to explore what's possible. They will need less direction than their early-career colleagues. Ensuring they have ample resources is often assumed and therefore overlooked.

Additional Tips for Managers

- Once you move someone into a new role (or hire someone), don't test them all over again. In getting their footing, they need to believe that you believe they can be successful. Watch what you are mirroring. Tell your employees why you hired them. This will not only signal confidence, but help them uncover their why or their purpose.

- No matter how promising a person is, neither of you yet know if this is the right S Curve. Explorers have logs; Collectors collect and tag their specimens. Collect data: Where is a person on their current S Curve? Will this lead to achieving their long-term goals? Does the person have the necessary resources? Assess whether the current role or assignment is sufficiently novel that they have room to grow, but familiar enough, whether domain or relationship expertise, or both, that they can be successful. Continually evaluate momentum.

- Because of all the newness, to shore up a sense of identity, there can be a tendency to perform rather than to learn. Manage this by having your team set goals that are experiment-based (for example, what did you learn this week?) and process-oriented (for example, map out, meet, and serve your key stakeholders). Trust that behaviors, if practiced consistently, will lead to desired outcomes.

- Invest in frequent, honest communication: *It is either time consuming or uncomfortable or both to give you feedback, so when I do, I am investing in you.* As Jeff Lyman, former chief product officer at Weave, a communication platform for small and medium-sized businesses, said, his job is "vision and strategy, air cover, resourcing, and hard feedback."[1] Be concrete and specific, beginning with what is working. When someone knows exactly what is working, they can do more of it. Be clear about what isn't working so that individuals can quickly course correct. The tension between what is and what isn't working will allow people to make the quickest progress. While some people struggle with imposter syndrome and their perception of how well they are doing trails reality, for others, perception precedes reality. If you are invested in their development, you will give feedback. If you aren't—whether the feedback is positive or negative—it may be an indication you aren't invested.

- Watch for identity mismatch, overlap, and shadow values. If people are struggling in their role—consider to what extent it may be out of line with how they perceive themselves. Be willing to call out when people are collecting data about themselves that isn't true. If you are struggling to allow them to flourish, it may be that their emerging self feels like an incursion into the territory of your identity. If you are not willing to allow people to explore, get curious about why.

- For team members who would prefer to be the expert, to perpetually remain in mastery, and not be learners, emphasize that while their learning is your priority, it needs to be theirs too. We sometimes believe that if we say or do the right thing, if we create a fertile ecosystem for growth, then our people will engage. It's a both/and. You create conditions where growth is possible *and* your team members choose to grow.

- Encourage inner work. Technical skills are necessary but not sufficient for growth. To grow your company, your people need to grow their childlike skills of curiosity, wonder, and attention and become world-class Collectors of feedback.

- Practice gratitude. Publicly acknowledge and appreciate how the people on your team are growing. When you focus on and celebrate growth, you get more growth.

Grow Your Company: Launch Point Implications for Leaders

Following are specific, tactical ways to apply the S Curve of Learning model and the S Curve Insight Platform to grow your organization.[2]

- To orient your team for growth, the proportion of people on the launch point should be relatively small (that is, less than 20 percent) but significant enough to balance two factors: 1) ensure that the team can provide near-term efficient output; 2) counteract the tendency to have those on the launch point fit the mold of the existing team. Their newness can be a strength if you harness it properly, so help the whole team listen for how their fresh perspective can inform collective growth.

- Individuals on the launch point help provide the impetus to get your organization to the pinnacle of your S Curve. Their enthusiasm for the climb and their questioning helps you uncover opportunities for innovation—from products to process to people.

- One of the major benefits of bringing people in at the launch point is that they feel you've taken a chance on them. The reward and payoff can be loyalty, dedication, and hard work from those in whom you invest. There is an esprit de corps among teams that move up the Curve together successfully.

- Take stock of where your company is in its growth trajectory and what resources are available to support individuals on the launch point.

- Consider the impact of having a team heavily weighted at the launch point. If your organization has a disproportionate number of people at this point, the time and energy required to move people off the launch point is a worthy challenge, but it can deplete and exhaust leadership, as well as longer-tenured team members.

- If you don't currently have team members on the launch point, take a step back to grow. Create practices to ensure that you are collectively questioning the status quo.

PART TWO

SWEET SPOT

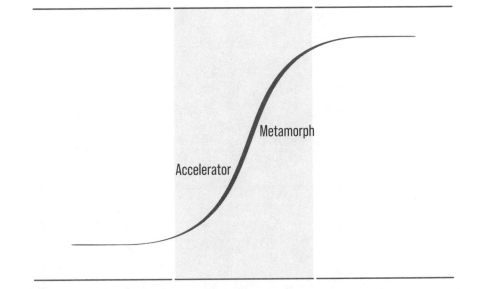

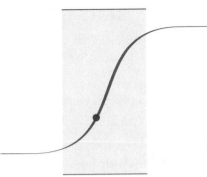

3 Accelerator

Because running fast is more fun than running slow.

—FRANK SHORTER

You are *here*.

In the sweet spot.

It often creeps up on you unawares. From "I'm stressed out; I can't do this," things gradually shift. Like waiting to recover from an illness and slowly improving but not really noticing, until one day, you are better. We notice pain much more readily than we notice improvement.

But now that you are here, something marvelous is happening in your brain: it's changing. When you understand how it's changing and why, you can grow even faster.

Our brains are more than mere processors—they're predictors. They are continuously running predictive models that govern all our conscious and unconscious actions, everything from typing the next keystroke to planning the next twenty years.

Running a predictive model requires a hypothesis: an expectation of what will happen. *If I read this book, I will get smarter.* Whether your behavior is deliberate or automatic, your brain constantly collects data to test hypotheses. What are my senses telling me? What is my intuition—my "gut"—telling me? Does this data confirm or disconfirm what I currently believe?

This is learning. There's a *physical* change in our brain (it's called neural plasticity) when we learn. Our amazing brain cells, the neurons, develop cell-to-cell connections called synapses. When we learn, new synapses form between cells that hadn't previously been connected. Think of it as a networking event in your brain. ("Hello, my name is Neuron." "No kidding! That's my name, too.") Every time you take a breath or think a thought, you are calling your neurons and their synapses to action.

The rate at which our synaptic network grows is a function of how often we do things that challenge our brains. New learning outside our ordinary comfort zone takes extra effort, and mental effort translates into faster neuronal growth. As Terry Sejnowski, a professor at the Salk Institute for Biological Studies in San Diego, described to me, "We need to acquire some stress."[1] The learning stress we acquire provides new cells and circuitry, which can be put to work for our brains' predictive modeling.

The results of the predictions produce a physical reaction—specifically the release of dopamine, the chemical messenger that makes us feel delight. When you make a prediction and get it wrong, your unmet expectations lead to a drop in dopamine. You are less able to feel good; you may even feel bad. If you get what you expect, you experience little to no increase in dopamine. Exceeded expectations generate a large increase in dopamine. As you might guess, the brain catalogs these reactions and seeks the dopamine reward of exceeding expectations.

When you strike out on a new S Curve, you may be accustomed to a predictable, ho-hum level of dopamine. Your brain has its expectations. But as you, a creature of habit, become a creature in the wild—an Explorer, a Collector—your lack of experience leaves wide gaps in your predictive model. You will run up against unmet expectations as you attempt new things. Unmet expectations don't feel good. That's part of why the launch point of an S Curve can feel like a slog. Slow.

The sweet spot, by contrast, is characterized by increasingly accurate (but not *too* accurate) predictive models, together with increasingly more and more dopamine rewards. It's the upside surprise that gives you the frisson of excitement. The sweet surprise fast-tracks the formation of neural connections. Dopamine is teaching you what is and isn't working. *Fast*.

The connection between dopamine and neural growth highlights the marvelous plasticity of our brains. Brains can change. *We* can change them. We can alter our hypotheses. We can add new inputs. We can produce different outcomes. We can choose smart growth.

Welcome to the Sweet Spot

Accelerator is the third phase along your S Curve of Learning. You have now collected the data and resources you need, committed to an S Curve, and tipped into the sweet spot of your growth. There are fewer gaps in your knowledge, and you have a good sense of where the remaining gaps lie. You're making conscious, deliberate choices about how you want to grow, and those choices become more automatic as stress and growth approach equilibrium. It's fun! You feel the exhilaration that comes with conquering your challenges, with managing yourself.

Jeremy Andrus is a serial entrepreneur, currently CEO of Traeger Grills. Backyard chefs know Traeger as the grill that burns hardwood pellets instead of charcoal or gas—without having to chop wood. Patented in 1986 by amateur inventor Joe Traeger, the pellet grill gained a niche following.

When I sat down with Andrus in late 2019, he'd had a particularly busy week.[2] As he got home one night around 10 p.m. after a business dinner, his wife, Kristin, asked him how his day had been. He said, "Today was crazy and chaotic and hard, but it was awesome. I loved it." That, to me, is the sweet spot.

At forty-two, Andrus was the former wunderkind of Skullcandy, maker of cool headphones and audio accessories. He was initially reluctant about Traeger; he had no experience in the grill business. But when he started collecting data, he found something compelling. "As I spoke to Traeger grill owners, there was a level of passion that I've never seen in a consumer product before," he says. "They didn't say it was the best grill they'd ever owned, it was the best *product* they had ever owned."[3] But despite the magic in this twenty-seven-year-old brand, the company hadn't scaled. Andrus's interest was piqued.

It quickly became clear why Traeger hadn't accelerated: its whole operation was costly and inefficient. Traeger was still performing tasks in-house that its competitors had outsourced years before. Given the strength of its product and brand, overhauling operations should give the company the lift it needed.

It was an S Curve too tempting to resist; Andrus took the CEO job. He quickly learned that the operational issues paled in comparison to Traeger's culture, which was deeply hostile toward change. Seven CEOs had come and gone in rapid succession, each defeated by Traeger's toxic culture. No one was able to turn the company around. Andrus was number eight.

> Later on I learned that employees called me Ocho (Spanish for *eight*) behind my back. They didn't expect me to last long. Their behavior reflected that. When I asked for data, they would ignore me. I'd ask people to work together on a project, and they'd simply refuse. Once, when I was visiting headquarters, I asked the CFO if he could meet with me. Even though I was his boss, he said he couldn't find any time in his schedule.

The launch point of his Traeger CEO S Curve was painful. His first step was to buy out the majority shareholder, who was holding the company hostage in 1980s operations. Andrus said, "It was an important moment—one we celebrate as a company holiday every year. We call it Traeger Independence Day." The second step was to upgrade warehouses and outsource trucking operations. Andrus knew that meant layoffs, and he agonized over the decision. Predictably, he faced considerable resistance from Traeger's old guard. "Toxic culture" took on new meaning: "I pulled into the parking lot at my office to find it surrounded by fire trucks. One of our big-rig trucks was on fire. We didn't know who was responsible, but it was obviously arson."

Andrus was sympathetic toward the employees that would have to be laid off if Traeger meant to modernize and grow. He knew they were hurt. He was offering generous severance payouts. But an employee barbequing a company truck was too much. Traeger needed serious restructuring before somebody got hurt. He moved headquarters from Oregon to Utah. Only a fraction of the employees came along.

The Utah move was Traeger's tipping point into the sweet spot. Acceleration followed. Soon operations were cooking. Sales exploded. Legacy culture gave way to a spirit of camaraderie on the new campus where employees were flipping burgers at a home office stocked with Traeger grills.

When Andrus joined me on my *Disrupt Yourself* podcast, you could have called him *Siete*—as in seven years at the helm of Traeger during which revenue went from $70 million to half a billion and climbing.[4] Andrus shared his own recipe for smart growth: "Reset, swing big, and make sure you have a team that's as good as the size of your vision."

We Have Liftoff

I enjoy watching footage of the 1969 Saturn V rocket, the pioneering craft that launched the first moonwalkers into space. It is an apt metaphor for the S Curve of Learning. For all the elegance of its engineering, the Saturn V's liftoff looks a bit clumsy: like trying to get a high-rise building off the ground. The massive first-stage engines generated more than 7.5 million pounds of thrust, yet it took a slow twelve seconds for the 3,100-ton rocket to clear its own launch tower.[5]

Acceleration didn't begin in earnest until roughly thirty-eight miles up, when the second-stage engines fired and the first-stage engines dropped away. Then the ungainly phase was over. Stage two was over thirteen times more fuel efficient and reached a speed three times faster than stage one.

When we reach the acceleration stage in the sweet spot of the S Curve of Learning, the gawkiness of exploration and collection is likewise complete. We are increasingly productive, competent, and confident. Our stage-two rockets have fired. Serious acceleration is underway.

Racing along the S: C + A + R

Motivation to continue and confidence in the outcome are hallmarks of people in the Accelerator phase. Jeremy Andrus currently exemplifies this.

"We're swinging big," he told me. "I love the problems we are solving and I'm confident we can solve them."

According to self-determination theory, our needs for the following are being fulfilled:[6]

Competence

Autonomy

Relatedness

We'll use the acronym CAR as a mnemonic device.

Choose a favorite car to use in the acceleration phase of your S Curve. Maybe the Accelerator you imagine is a Lamborghini, a Ferrari, or a Porsche. Or maybe you prefer a vintage muscle car or a 4×4 truck. Perhaps it's a Tesla or some other peppy electric vehicle. Visualize your ideal car.

Now, imagine driving it. Maybe you're navigating breathtaking curves on the Pacific Coast Highway, California's iconic coastal highway, enjoying the ocean views. The power at your feet is exhilarating. The salt air breeze off the ocean carries the scent of adventure.

C Is for Competence

You are enjoying this because of the *competence* you've acquired. You're not a sixteen-year-old, first learning to drive. You know what you're doing, completely at ease behind the wheel.

When you're in the sweet spot, you experience equilibrium: You're competent and things are getting easier, but not so easy that you're bored and complacent. You know what you know. You have a good grasp of what you *don't* know. The sweet spot is full of challenges that hone your predictive models. "Is everything working?" Jeremy Andrus asked, speaking of Traeger. "No. We have a thousand problems. But we have a strategy, and we have an unbelievable platform of people who can help us solve those problems."

In 2018, Traeger confronted a major problem. Steel prices soared with new tariffs on goods imported from China. Lower-cost competitors edged into Traeger's territory. Growth was ominously slow. Traeger faced a risky choice: double down on branding and emphasize the quality of its products or hunker down and cut costs to keep up with the interest on its debt. It could swing big or bunt.

Andrus, in full Accelerator mode, chose to swing for the fences. He knew he was competent enough to face the crisis, because he'd already been thrown this S Curve at Skullcandy. Consumer spending slumped at a time when Skullcandy's competitors were carving into the millennial demographic, armed with similar products and hip branding. "We went from white-hot to, painfully, 'how do we eke out growth and profitability?' And I didn't know how to reset."

With Traeger, Andrus knew how. At the time, Traeger was inventing a line of reasonably priced grill-smoker hybrids. Best of all, they were Wi-Fi and Bluetooth enabled. "Set it and forget it" was the catchphrase. Traeger decided to bet on the tech-savvy demographic: cooks who could keep a watchful eye on the grill from an app.[7] "We took a really big risk on launching a connected product at a relatively low price point," Andrus told me, "but [appealing to millennials] was an important risk to take."

Andrus has the hallmarks of a smart growth leader. He's been at the wheel of his car a time or two around the track, he knows when to hit the gas and when to put on the brakes; he knows how to course correct. He also knows that to grow Traeger, he needs to grow himself. When asked about his Skullcandy experience, Andrus says he feels nothing but deep, deep gratitude because of what he learned. He says, "I'm in the middle of these incredibly difficult situations and they don't feel like a burden to me. They feel fun."

A Is for Autonomy

The A in CAR is autonomy, which Accelerators require. Autonomy equals choice. We govern ourselves. We legislate our lives. We have the power to choose. Determined Accelerators find autonomy even when circumstances seem to offer little in the way of choice.

Let's revisit the story of Astrid Tuminez from the introduction. Even in the slums of her childhood upbringing in the Philippines, choices were still available to her. Nuns in Iloilo City made school available to her for free, and she chose to take advantage of that. She chose to work hard. "Because I had access to a library at school, I got to read magazines like *Time* and *Newsweek*. I made the decision quite early that I would go to the United States, that I would live in New York, and that I would work for the United Nations because I read about it in *Time* magazine." And she did.[8]

Astrid Tuminez couldn't choose to be born in a family where getting a US visa was a forgone conclusion. She couldn't shape US immigration policy. Her visa applications were twice denied. "You're young, you're poor," she was told. "You're an immigration risk. Don't come."

But Tuminez could choose to tap into her human resources.[9] Her network of friends and mentors opened the doors that circumstances shut. There were people who would vouch for her character and potential. The third time, she got a visa. "Coming to the US was incredibly liberating," she says. America gave Tuminez more freedom than she had ever known.

Fortunately, autonomy doesn't entirely hinge on the level of freedom granted to us by others. Even for those fortunate enough to live in wealthy democracies, not all circumstances will offer an abundance of choice. Autonomy also depends on our willingness to act rather than to be acted upon and to own the consequences of our actions. Astrid Tuminez was living in a slum in Iloilo City, and still she managed to be an Accelerator.

Sometimes the fuel in our accelerating CAR runs a little low. Liz O'Donnell, for example, encountered a crisis of autonomy when her aging parents began to require extra care.[10] O'Donnell is chief content officer at Double Forte, a public relations firm and the author of *Working Daughter: A Guide to Caring for Your Aging Parents*. In 2020, she told me, "I remember the exact moment that *Working Daughter* came to me." It was on a vacation day she had scheduled because her mother needed to visit the doctor. O'Donnell's "vacation" began at 6 a.m., fielding work emails. She got her two children off to school. Then came the doctor's appointment with her mom:

> The doctor grilled me. He wanted to know why I didn't know how much my mother was eating and why I wasn't calling her every day. He asked me, right in front of my mother, "Why haven't you moved her in with you yet?" He stopped just shy of asking me why I was still working.

The growing demands in O'Donnell's life were both logistical and emotional. In a phase of life where she might have been accelerating, there wasn't enough time to grow in her career, not enough time to spend with her young family. Even greater challenges followed. O'Donnell's mother and father were diagnosed with terminal illnesses, both on the same day.

O'Donnell candidly shared how she felt at first. "I really resented it," she told me. "I was a working mom. I only had so many hours with my children." Her choices were now more limited. The cost of being there for her ailing parents was going to be high, but the opportunity was greater: to be present at the end of their lives. That recognition was a turning point. She says, "I thought, *The only way through this is through this. So stop fighting it and get it done.*"

O'Donnell's let's-do-this attitude was a choice. With her choice came confidence. The sweet spot is not mere happenstance; it's a place you choose to be. Right here. Right now.

O'Donnell learned that she had autonomy, even when it wasn't obvious. She was in the driver's seat. What began as a compulsory new S Curve of Learning ("I have to deal with this because no one else can") developed into an autonomous S Curve ("I choose to be here at the end of my parents' lives"). Even when unforeseen circumstances limit our autonomy, "we can hold two truths at the same time," O'Donnell said. "We can hold one truth, which is 'this is hell, and I don't want to do it,' and the other truth which is 'I know that this is a phenomenal moment, and I love that I'm able to care for my parents.'"

Organizations can accelerate through autonomy, too. In 2014, engineers at the Indian automotive company Mahindra & Mahindra had come up with an idea for a full-fledged SUV: the Scorpio. They presented a crude clay model of their brainchild to executives at Ford, a partner company they hoped would back them on it. They talked about their development budget. They wanted Ford to guide the process and make Scorpio a reality. Ford was impressed. "Right away," recalls CEO Anand Mahindra, "the vice chairman of the company offered . . . a team of seasoned Ford engineers to assist us. . . . At that point, the chairman interjected and said, 'No, let's not send any engineers at all. If we do, this vehicle may come out looking like a Ford car and costing just as much. If these guys can really develop this car they've just shown us at the cost they claim they can, then I think we are the ones who should be learning from them.'"

Mahindra took the wheel. The Scorpio has sold more than a half-million units since its rollout. Mahindra said, "I owe Ford a debt of gratitude for leaving us to fend for ourselves. Because when I look back upon these events, I know that the choice Ford made [not to partner on the Scorpio] put us solidly on the path of self-reliance. But I admit that I have often wondered how things would have turned out had Ford made a different choice. What if they had not abandoned us to do the Scorpio alone? We would not have built the capabilities we possess today."[11]

As Accelerators, we have the skills we need (competence), we have the power to make choices, and we choose to be on this S Curve (autonomy). That leaves *R*, *relatedness*, which is the recognition that we are interconnected and that we belong.

R Is for Relatedness

Priyanka Carr and Gregory Walton conducted a study that demonstrates the power of relatedness.[12] Subjects met in groups and then were separated and tasked with solving puzzles alone. One group, the "psychologically together" group, was told that they were still working as a team to solve their puzzle, and they would receive "a tip from a team member." A second group heard nothing about teamwork.

All participants were, in fact, working alone regardless of what they were told. But people in the psychologically together category worked 48 percent longer, solved more problems correctly, and had better recall for what they had seen. They also said that they felt less tired and depleted by the task and reported finding the puzzle more interesting.[13]

Accelerators work together, and as important, they *feel* as if they are part of a team.

Zaza Pachulia, a retired two-time NBA champion, told me that during his career, it was rare to find an NBA rookie who put his team first.[14] Rookies want to prove themselves as individuals, a mindset that can result in selfish play. Over time, most players come to realize that they won't be at their best unless the team is at *its* best. The team is more likely to win.

Pachulia learned this during his 2013–2015 seasons with the Milwaukee Bucks. His coach was Jason Kidd, new to the job after a legendary career as an NBA point guard. Some pundits derided Kidd as "the worst coach in the NBA" after a gaffe-ridden first year as head coach for the Brooklyn Nets.[15] But Kidd pushed through his early setbacks to become a Coach of the Year candidate in 2015 when he turned Pachulia's Bucks into a contending team.

Kidd taught Pachulia that you have to be able to read what's about to happen as a play unfolds. "You can't read the court if you don't know the tendencies of your teammates," Pachulia told me, "their strengths, their weaknesses." Pachulia says that, for example, he "cannot jump," so it was pointless to throw him a high pass. A low pass followed by a hard drive to the paint offered better odds of scoring. Pachulia's teammates needed to understand his strengths and weaknesses to help him play most effectively.

When Pachulia and others talk about team "chemistry," they are, in essence, talking about team *relatedness*. Relatedness requires both a shared identity and a personal familiarity with other team members. Time on the road (half of a team's games are played on the road) gives players the opportunity to get to know each other off court. "That carries over onto the court," Pachulia says.

Team identity is basic to our biology, key to the survival of our highly communal human species. When we share an identity, we feel related. Relatedness accelerates our growth. In their landmark 1995 study, psychologists Roy Baumeister and Mark Leary write, "Human beings are fundamentally and pervasively motivated by a need to belong, that is, by a strong desire to form and maintain enduring interpersonal attachments."[16]

But interpersonal attachments and teamwork can be tough when our individual identities, interests, and incentives are battling with the shared identity, interests, and incentives of the group.

Conflict resolution expert, Donna Hicks, joined my *Disrupt Yourself* podcast in 2018. She is a scholar with experience in bringing adversaries to the table in some of the thorniest conflicts in the Middle East.[17] Hicks explained that when we believe another person is standing in the way of our needs or our interests, deep down we believe they're standing in the way of our basic human dignity—our inherent value and worth.

You can protect the dignity of others, thus disarming their conflict response, by fostering relatedness. That starts with shared experiences (like playing on the same team) and nonconflicting goals (like winning an NBA championship).[18] When drawing upon shared experience, we feel safely connected to someone. We use the same part of the brain for thinking about their experience as we do for thinking about our own.[19] It releases oxytocin, the empathy hormone. We conclude someone is a friend; we affix the *friend* label. Without shared goals, our brain functions differently. We attach a *foe* label. A foe's thoughts are not our thoughts: less empathy, less oxytocin, less relatedness. Whether we're in a boardroom or a locker room, we require relatedness to accelerate and maintain the momentum of the sweet spot.[20]

One more thought as we complete our lap around the confidence track: the S Curve of Learning model itself increases confidence. It maps to where you are in your growth journey (competency), sets you as the driver of your growth (autonomy), and it gives you a shared language for growth (relatedness).

C + A + R = Competence + Autonomy + Relatedness = Confidence.

Cooking with Confidence

Ellen Bennett, a Mexican American entrepreneur, started out as a restaurant line cook. In 2012, Bennett was working her way up the food chain at a two-Michelin-starred restaurant. Nobody knew that the twenty-four-year-old sauteing the onions was also dreaming big. Bennett had acquired a California business license, bent on starting her own culinary clothing company. "I felt so legit and official," she laughingly told me. Her business plan? Nonexistent. "I didn't even know when, or where, or how I was going to do it," she said.

What she *did* know was (a) how to sew aprons; and (b) that the aprons they were wearing in the kitchen were terrible. "I realized that our gear stunk. It was bad. It didn't fit well, it didn't look good on men, women, you name it. It just was terrible." Her boss knew it too. A vendor was supplying new aprons, he said. Did she want one? Bennett said,

In that split second, I blurted out "Chef, I have an apron company. I will make the aprons." He said, "What are you talking about? You're a line cook in my kitchen." "No, you don't understand. I've been doing business. This is going to be amazing. We're going to make you the best aprons ever."

Just like that, Bennett went from line cook to supplier with a forty-apron contract. "I convinced him right there on the spot to give me this order." Could she single-handedly crank out the first batch in her after hours? She could. "You better believe I delivered the aprons."

The aprons were terrible.

Bennett continued, "He [my boss] said, 'Bennett, these aprons suck. The straps are falling off.' I almost died right then and there. I could have just thrown in the towel and said, 'I'm sorry. I'll give you your money back. But instead, I decided to take control of what had happened and make it right. And so I did."

Back to the sewing machine. She delivered better aprons, and a company was born. In less than ten years, her scrappy startup—Hedley & Bennett—has accelerated to sell millions of dollars of products. This is the sweet spot for a CEO who hasn't even turned forty. She's got confidence to produce a quality product, uses her autonomy to own the failures as well as the success, and helps her employees—and her business—grow with positive relatedness. Getting here has involved some disasters: the raw panic of realizing a big shipment wouldn't make its deadline, the misery of telling a major client their order is going unfilled. Bennett said, "And yet I look back and I think about my chef with the straps, I took responsibility at that moment. And it helped me just learn that that was part of the journey."

Predicting How You're Going to Succeed

Outcomes were unpredictable when Ellen Bennett was first growing her business, before she hit her sweet spot. Remembering a big order she got from a high-value client, she said, "It was monumental volumes of stress by the minute, seeing there was an iceberg in front of us, and I couldn't steer the ship in the right direction." Now in the sweet spot, her predictive model is more accurate. She feels more certain.

Certainty makes you feel you're in control. You have more autonomy. You're in a fast CAR, you're the driver, and you've got the pedal down. But even when your predictions aren't perfect, your S Curve of Learning road map gives your brain a hack for hanging onto that "I'm crushing it!" feeling. You know where you are on your S Curve, and you know where you're going.

One of the things I learned from my career in finance was that if you start and finish strong—if you get your buy and sell decisions right—everything in between (the sweet spot, for example) takes care of itself.

Since 1857, the average return for the stock market in the United States has been 5 percent. If you had invested $100 then, it would now be worth $300,000.

But let's say you didn't just invest the $100 and forget about the money. Instead, every four-and-a-half years, you sold your stocks before you went on a month-long vacation and bought them back at the end of your vacation.

If, during your vacation, the market performed poorly, then your average return would be 9 percent. This doesn't sound like much except that we are talking about compounding returns, so your $100 is now worth $130 million.[21] However, if the market performed well while you were on vacation, the average return would be 1 percent, and the $100 would be worth only $800.

Myron Scholes, the Nobel Prize–winning financial economist who conducted this research, says, "All of the returns are explained by the tails [the beginning and the ending]. The middle is a lot of noise."[22]

Of course, even the savviest investor can never time their buying and selling perfectly. But let's apply the idea (loosely) to our growth.

Every S Curve has a beginning, a middle, and an end: launch point, sweet spot, and mastery. Getting smart about our growth means learning to manage through the entire growth cycle. If we frame our curves correctly, get our beginnings (the launch point decisions) and endings (the moves we make when we are in the mastery phase) right, the sweet spot can then have an automaticity. It is not that there is no work to do in the middle; far from it. There are strategies we can employ that help to wring maximum value from the sweet spot—the subject of the next chapter. Broadly, however, many of the middle details will take care of themselves, leaving us free to enjoy the ride. Recall the Saturn rocket; once the stage two rockets fire, the Saturn accelerates. Once it breaks free of the constraint of earth's gravity, its momentum is maintained by the gravitational pull of the moon. Obviously, there are still complexities, but the heavy lift is over, until it's time to land the lunar module on the moon.

Every Day Is an S Curve

In my previous book, *Build an A-Team*, I talked about optimizing individuals on their S Curves to build a high-performing, innovative team. I posited that the standard bell curve distribution percentages of about 15 percent of team members on the launch point, 70 percent in the sweet spot, and 15 percent in mastery are a solid baseline.[23]

What if we applied similar math to every day of our lives? As if each new morning were the launch point of an S Curve, and we spent most of our day confidently in the sweet spot, feeling competent, autonomous, related—and exhilarated? Remember what Jeremy Andrus said of his acceleration at Traeger: "I love every single day of this. Today was crazy and chaotic and hard, but it was awesome. I loved it."

It's worth aiming for 15 percent (approximately) of each day spent at the high end, automatically performing tasks that we've fully mastered. Another 15 percent spent on the launch point, grappling with problems that are a bit more taxing, even a little beyond our reach. Fifteen percent seems like a magical amount; remember we're also looking for about 15 percent novelty on a new S Curve, and 85 percent familiarity (Explorer, chapter 1).

Our goal could be to spend most of each day in the sweet spot. When you're in the sweet spot—whether on a yearslong quest for growth, or just trying to maximize the potential of a single day—you can spend more of your time *being*, not just *doing*. Seizing and savoring the moment. It's been almost three decades since Mihaly Csikszentmihalyi published his groundbreaking work, *Flow: The Psychology of Optimal Experience*.[24] The concept of flow has been applied to myriad situations and states of mind since. Spending part of each day in a sweet spot is what I think of as equivalent to flow. Csikszentmihalyi writes:

> There are people who, regardless of their material conditions, have been able to improve the quality of their lives, who are satisfied, and who have a way of making those around them also a bit more happy. Such individuals lead vigorous lives, are open to a variety of experiences, keep on learning until the day they die, and have strong ties and commitments to other people and to the environment in which they live. They enjoy whatever they do, even if tedious or difficult; they are hardly ever bored, and they can take in stride anything that comes their way. Perhaps their greatest strength is that they are in control of their lives.[25]

Control is elusive, but highly sought. Perhaps control eludes us because we are almost always looking ahead, trying to ensure control of future outcomes rather than making the most of the moment. Try instead to make each day an optimal experience. Spend more of your life in the sweet spot by spending more of each day in the sweet spot. Tomorrow is always headed our way; it will become today soon enough.

Accelerator Takeaways

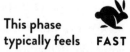

This phase typically feels **FAST**

The third stage of your S-Curve of Learning is called Accelerator, when you reach the sweet spot phase and the pace of your growth accelerates. You are here because of the hard work you did in the launch phase, including the initial learning, data collection, and decision making. The first stage of the S Curve's sweet spot is marked by an increasing ability to produce more results with less effort, increased accuracy of your brain's predictive model, and a feeling of exhilaration. You have liftoff and have moved from *slow* to *fast*. Your pace up the S Curve has quickened and you are still picking up speed.

This stage in your smart growth consists of motivation to grow and the confidence that you can. According to self-determination theory, your needs for competence, autonomy, and relatedness are being met. Use the mnemonic device (CAR) as you accelerate.

The CAR Model

- **Competence.** Now that you've crossed over into the sweet spot, you are increasingly capable of producing results. You start to experience an equilibrium: progress toward your goal is getting easier, but not so easy as to create boredom and complacency. The data collection and decision making you completed on the launch point has strengthened your mind's predictive capacity. You can now take on new challenges with a better understanding of what the results are likely to be.

- **Autonomy.** Autonomy speeds up your acceleration. Note that this is *not* the "I'm alone and doing this by myself" type of autonomy, but rather the kind that harnesses your internal power to take responsibility, make decisions, and solve problems. Your sense of autonomy is strengthened when you know you've made a difference and is weakened if others are doing the work or making the key decisions for you. Successful Accelerators find ways to move forward even when circumstances offer limited options.

- **Relatedness.** Vibrant connection to something larger than yourself is the third component of your CAR. This relatedness involves two dimensions: the sense that you are connected (for example, contributing to a compelling vision, part of a larger effort) and the experience of belonging to a team or group. Relatedness is a basic human need and essential for maintaining momentum along the curve. We'll talk about this in depth in chapter 7, Ecosystem.

In the Accelerator stage, difficult situations can actually be fun, as you have sufficient knowledge and resources to make things happen. It may feel like things are going smoothly, and this is normal. When work feels more hard than fun, be persistent to sustain momentum. You can make a conscious choice to stay and grow in the sweet spot—enjoy the flow.

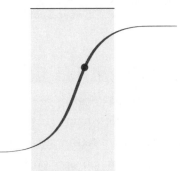

4 Metamorph

I may not be there yet, but I am closer than I was yesterday.

—MISTY COPELAND

Maria Merian (the seventeenth-century naturalist you first met in chapter 2) was fascinated by insect metamorphosis. Her paintings capture caterpillars, chrysalises, and the final "winged jewels" flourishing in their native ecosystems.

In this chapter we'll explore metamorphosis too—not of insects, but of ourselves. The S Curve of Learning changes you. Much of your metamorphosis happens in the sweet spot, and it tends to be thrilling. Maybe you're seeing your product hit the shelves, your client list get longer and longer, the ribbon cut at your brand-new storefront, or the hiring letter of your dreams. But that's not all that's changing. Look past the outward bustle. Look at what's happening inside you as well.

Your metamorphosis began at the launch point. Whether you call yourself a butterfly or a water lily, the principle is the same. You, at some point, began to believe in your own potential, to believe your goals were within reach. That belief grew inside you. Like a caterpillar preparing to fly or a lily stem striving toward the pond surface, you inched forward at the bottom of your S Curve, collecting resources and experience. Subtly, and then suddenly, you've picked up speed. What was unfamiliar behavior is becoming automatic. The sweet spot is the chrysalis of your identity. "I do this" evolves into "I am this."

You are now a *Metamorph*.

It sounds like a superhero name. It should, because it captures the unique human superpower of getting smart about your growth, of becoming something greater than you previously were. As a Metamorph, you have resources available and have the competence to utilize them, but you still have considerable room to grow.

Michelle McKenna is probably an actual superhero and definitely a Metamorph. McKenna is chief information officer (CIO) of the mighty National Football League (NFL).[1]

Before coming to the NFL, McKenna was the CIO of Constellation Energy, a major US electricity generator. In 2012, as Constellation was merging with nuclear power giant Exelon, McKenna's job required a move to Chicago. "I didn't want to move to Chicago," McKenna told me, "but I didn't want to look for another job."

Then came a happy coincidence. She said, "I am a huge sports fan. I was on the [NFL's] Fantasy Football site and there was a link to 'About Us', and then there was one for jobs. I opened it, and it was the CIO position. They didn't call it a CIO, but when I read the description I thought, 'They need a CIO.'"

McKenna would have to convince the NFL to morph the role from what they thought it was—VP of IT—to what she knew it should be. She said, "What they really needed was to upgrade the position—make it a senior vice president, give the person a seat at the table."

It took six months of shuttling between Baltimore and New York, but the NFL finally hired her. NFL commissioner Roger Goodell was supportive. McKenna said, "He said to me over and over, 'You sold me, but now have to sell it to everybody else. Nobody around here knows what a CIO is. We've never had one of you before.'"

As predicted, McKenna's colleagues were dubious, constantly questioning the need for her in meetings. She remembers them telling her, "You're supposed to keep the data center up and the phones running—why are you here?" Watercooler oddsmakers were betting she wouldn't be there long.

But McKenna beat the odds and hit the sweet spot. She built a close-knit team, developing the relatedness we talked about in the previous chapter. She rolled out next-generation technology, like GPS devices on player equipment to trace their movements on the field. McKenna may have started out in IT, but she has ended up transforming NFL operations. After eight years, one might conclude that McKenna had little room left to grow. But along came Covid-19. Professional sports reeled, and early in the pandemic the NFL suspended the 2020 season.[2] Teams instructed coaches and scouts to cancel their travel plans. Meanwhile, the league was only six weeks away from its annual draft: a high-stakes, three-day ritual where teams vie for the most promising new players. Pundits predict and speculate, team managers strategize, and fans expect pomp and ceremony in front of the cameras. McKenna and her team had been working for months to orchestrate a live event for 200,000-plus fans in Las Vegas. And now she couldn't even leave her house.

In business, as in football, sometimes you have to scramble. McKenna teamed up with events executive vice president Peter O'Reilly to solicit ideas from all quarters of the NFL. Junior personnel provided some of the best input (as Explorers and Collectors often do). But employees on their launch point also need leadership. As the days raced by with no decisions made, McKenna, in her sweet spot, stepped in. "'Stop,' she told everybody, 'I'm making a call. By tomorrow at 5:00 p.m., we'll decide which way we're going.'"

They settled on a virtual draft format. Key stakeholders at first found the concept distasteful to say the least. Draft prospects were deflated to learn they were "going to miss their red carpet." Coaches and general managers didn't want to be on camera in their living rooms. They didn't want to conduct critical business with unfamiliar tech. I interviewed Jason Licht, general manager of the Tampa Bay Buccaneers (the team that ultimately won the Super Bowl at the end of the 2020–2021 season), and he said, "I had a lot of general manager angst. How do I do this without my scouts, without my coaches next to me? How do I execute trades? Communicate with the owners?" And, "What if there's a power failure?"

McKenna describes the virtual draft as the most challenging project of her career: "The shortest time frame with the highest expectations. It wasn't the hardest technically, once we figured out how to technically do it. But it was very hard from a change management, expectation management, and how-we-were-going-to-make-it-something-the-NFL-could-be-very-proud-of perspective." But, she says, that was also what made it the most rewarding.

The results were astonishing, a metamorphosis for McKenna and for her organization. This draft turned out to be the most watched, possibly the most *loved*, draft in NFL history. More than 8 million viewers tuned in, millions of them stuck at home and desperate for an escape. The press raved about it. Broadcasting a huge event on live TV is a frantic affair under the best of circumstances; yet virtually everyone in the business agreed the virtual draft was the least glitchy since the event was first televised in 1980. Fans didn't find the intimacy of seeing players and pundits at home (plus occasional dogs and kids unexpectedly darting on screen) to be a turnoff. They saw NFL insiders suffering through lockdown just like everybody else. Licht said it was the least stressful draft he'd participated in since he became a general manager, "I wasn't interrupted with minutiae that a GM typically deals with. I was in the comfort of my home, kids in the living room, a few steps away, sharing the experience." Constraints, challenges, and stretch assignments offer opportunities to lengthen the sweet spot of the S Curve.

This eleventh-hour virtual draft was another transformation for smart growth leader Michelle McKenna—a micro curve within the sweet spot of her macro curve. McKenna draws on resources, from logistical and technical expertise to relationship capital, to grow herself, to grow her people, to grow the NFL.

First Focus. Then Fly

Extreme complexity and the very short time frame McKenna had to pull this off called for a heroic level of focus. When we are growing fast and changing, along the steepest part of the curve, focusing on how and why and in what direction we are trying to grow can prevent distraction and diversion.

I've been concentrating on focus for the past year, and it's a major theme in this book because smart growth requires it. Part of moving up the S Curve of Learning in my life has involved expanding my network and engaging with more ideas and opportunities. This results in a larger stream of constant input to my brain. On the surface, more input seems like a good thing, and it can be—a bigger pond, more lily pads. But it can also lead to too many ideas to choose between and work on. Cognitive overload coupled with anxiety can parasitically absorb our brain's resources just to cope with the stress.

As Metamorphs, we need to be deliberate about what we focus on to complete our transformation. "Focus on the positive," says behavior change expert Richard Boyatzis. "This activates our parasympathetic nervous system, sometimes referred to as the 'rest and digest' nervous system."[3] A slow and steady heart rate frees up resources that can be used to help grow neurons. Growth need not be a vague theoretical idea; it is made concrete in the anatomical structure of the brain.

Conversely, when we concentrate on what is not working well, the sympathetic nervous system (fight or flight) is activated. It's meant to warn us of danger and prepare us to react. Threatening situations might get us to pay attention, which is better than mindlessness, but we grow faster neurologically when we emphasize the positive.

Without sufficient focus, we won't complete the Metamorph stage of the S Curve. Distraction is our nemesis. We all have our favorites, but an almost universal distraction is watching television. Mihaly Csikszentmihalyi (who you met in Accelerator, chapter 3) pointed out that "TV watching leads to the flow condition very rarely. In fact, working people achieve the flow experience—deep concentration, high and balanced challenges and skills, a sense of control and satisfaction—about *four times as often* in their jobs, proportionately, as they do when they are watching television."[4] Thus our workspaces can be one of the best places to accomplish our own metamorphosis.

Even short distractions can lead to being *diverted* from our purpose. Our actions have a reliable tendency to follow what our eyes follow, and what occupies our brains (that's why the action board discussed in chapter 2 can work). Diversion puts us on a different path than we are trying to pursue, a different S Curve maybe, or a dead end, or a journey of aimless wandering.

To be fair to distraction, it's not *all* bad. In evolutionary terms, distraction is a survival mechanism: part of our brain is poised to barge in and alert us to the unexpected. We need this if, say, a wild boar just popped out of the underbrush with intent to charge. But that's not likely to happen in your office. Distraction at work is more likely to break your focus, deplete your resources, and leave you to get mauled by a deadline, not a boar. To avert wild-boar deadlines and keep up your momentum in the sweet spot, try some of these smart growth techniques.

Stay in the Moment

In *Star Wars Episode V*, the fictional Jedi master Yoda has his three-fingered hands full instructing his pupil Luke Skywalker to be in the moment. The location: a remote swamp. Young Luke is teetering in a handstand—and little wonder. His challenge is to simultaneously stack rocks one atop the other by means of the mysterious telekinetic ability known as the Force. "Concentraaaate!" Yoda exhorts. Luke collapses instead. "All his life has he looked away," Yoda later muses, "to the future, to the horizon. Never his mind on where he was, what he was doing."

It takes practice not to look away, no matter who you are. For Michelle McKenna, not every task associated with the virtual draft was interesting or invigorating, nor was emotional support readily available. She was both an empty nester and a young widow. She spent the early pandemic mostly alone. Days: monumental project management. Nights: details. Media kits had to be assembled and sent to nearly two hundred draft prospects, coaches (college and NFL), team owners, and general managers.[5] McKenna's evenings were filled with boxes, labels, and FedEx drops. She was facing a voracious deadline. Eventually her son arrived and took over assembly; friends left meals on her porch. Media kits (and meals) could have become major distractions. Loneliness could have, too. But McKenna stayed in the moment. She adapted, she delegated, she stayed on task.

Some tasks were invigorating. Orchestrating the virtual draft meant McKenna was the de facto TV director. The show was live on the air. She found herself doing something she'd never have dreamed of. Push camera one, ready camera two, make on-the-spot calls about who and what appeared on screen. To her own surprise, she loved it. With her mind on where she was, McKenna found herself on yet another micro curve.

Where is your mind? Stacking rocks of self-doubt? Sidetracked by the peripheral? Decidedly not! You are a Metamorph, and Metamorphs do not derail their productive flow. You can and will focus on the now. You will concentrate. You will grow wings.

Meditation can help us stay in the moment. But as Ellen Langer, a Harvard psychologist and longtime mindfulness researcher, says, "Meditation is something you engage in to lead to mindfulness. Mindfulness is an ongoing act in the moment, a way of being."[6] This is an important distinction. Meditation is an exercise; mindfulness is a way of being present. The majority of us spend most of our time *not* being present. Langer says, "When you're mindless, you're not able to take advantage of opportunities that present themselves. . . . You're not there and you're oblivious to not being there."

He's fictional, yes, but Yoda's assessment often applies to us. We're holding back our own metamorphosis when we aren't present where we are, living our own lives inside our own bodies, inside the moments we're given.

Langer teaches that a good place to start is simply paying more attention to what, and who, is right before us. We are mindfully engaged, Langer says, "by simply noticing new things." If you start looking for the unfamiliar in the familiar—if you make a point of noticing what you *don't* know, hidden amid the things you *do*—you'll stay in the moment. The moment will teach you. You will be able to get smarter about your growth.

In my office hang eight botanical drawings, primarily strawberries. As I shared with you in Collector (chapter 2), my husband grew up on a pick-your-own-berry farm in Maryland. In our current home, we also grow strawberries. For me, strawberries are home. But they have an additional symbolic meaning. Strawberries are whole, not sectioned or compartmentalized like an orange. The images of strawberries remind me not to let my attention become too compartmentalized, to keep my focus whole and on what is most important to me.

Triumph over Triggers

Some words, images, or ideas can trigger emotional distress. Emotional triggers are often rooted in past trauma, indelibly etched in memory, bringing fresh pain when forced into recall. Bad childhood memories are particularly stubborn. Emotional triggers can erode our confidence and leave us vulnerable to discouragement and depression. "I can't stop thinking about it," we might say. We may lose functionality at work or at home, as racing thoughts monopolize our energy. We can't go to sleep or stay asleep. We can't wake up. Triggers can upend our progress in the sweet spot and undermine our capacity to become a Metamorph. They are particularly devastating when they interrupt metamorphosis just as the chrysalis is beginning to crack.

Smart growth requires us to overcome patterns caused by triggers, such as seeking solace in addictive behavior or substances. Oftentimes triggers are linked back to shadow values, the values we talked about in the Explorer chapter, that are revealed by our default behavior. We espouse being a team player, but, in reality, we play to win at all costs. In this example, we could be triggered if we don't get a shout-out at the end of a big project we've worked hard on, even if it's an unintentional oversight. Absent the shadow value of needing to be recognized as a winner, we'd likely shrug our shoulders and say, "Whoops, forgot my name." If we do hold that shadow value, we could spend hours, days, even weeks harboring resentment, perseverating over what it means for our status, formulating a plan to redress this grievance, and so on.

I don't believe that any adult is trigger-free. Too many of us may have experienced some form of abuse and neglect, whether we realize it or not. Unresolved issues will bubble up from time to time, maybe frequently. When we have been triggered, it's important to acknowledge our feelings of loss and pain. There is no shame in expressing childlike grief, just as there is no shame in making childlike errors. This is a critical step in the healing process, often a step left undone when the formative trauma occurred. The pain of being unable to express what we felt at the time of the initial trauma may be proportional to a trigger's power to sabotage us in the present.

To deal with these emotional grenades, I ask myself questions like: *How would my future self* (meaning the person that I aspire to be) *react? Who do I want to be right now? How would someone who I admire hope I would respond in this situation?* If you are a person of faith, ask, *What course of action would my faith suggest?* Reframing and seeing the situation from a different perspective helps me right-size my response.

Here are two additional go-to techniques for deactivating triggers. First, I think about three things that I am grateful for right now, like the keyboard I am typing on, the hummingbird alighting on the feeder outside my window, and our cat Penelope lounging regally next to my computer. Expressing gratitude activates the parasympathetic nervous system and signals safety. The second practice, which I learned from psychologist Emma McAdam, is similar: immediately focus on three things I see, three things I hear, and three things I can touch.[7] The SWAT team of my physical senses helps subdue my reptilian, reactive brain. These mindful behaviors help me (and may help you too) stay in the moment, not in the memory.

Finally, the truth tellers in our orbits (including mental health professionals) can help us talk through triggering events and plan how to deal with them. It may take time, but we can triumph over what triggers us.

Just as the strength a butterfly musters in breaking out of the chrysalis is part of its metamorphosis, our learning to identify and defuse triggers will help us take flight.

Healthy Body, Sharp Mind

The whetstone that sharpens our mind is our body: what we eat, how we sleep, how we exercise.

Food, for example, manufactures the building blocks of our brain. Everything in our bodies is constructed of food, right down to our neurons. As health guru Shawn Stevenson said to me, "Food is your secret weapon." Intuitively and logically, we know it's true. But do we eat like we know it's true? Food can make us strong; all too often it makes us weak.

Research conducted on prison inmates suggests that having a bad diet is a better predictor of future violence than past violent behavior. Stevenson puts it bluntly: "You can predict bad behavior by what a person eats."[8] In sports, a diet of good, healthy food can be the difference between a gold medal and a participation trophy. Eat like a winner.

But here's where my twenty-year-old daughter would say we are going to do some real talk. As she frequently observes, and occasionally says out loud, when I am under stress (like on a deadline for a book), more than half the calories I consume come from something sweet. My nickname—Cookie Monster—is hard earned. When it comes to healthful eating, I frequently don't earn even a participation trophy.

The agony of adulthood is that we want to make these changes but feel we can't make them all at once; we are buried in work and stress; we struggle for ways to cope, to get by. If we can't make them all at once (and who can, really?), we may be paralyzed into no action at all. So if you're like me and most people, you know you ought to eat better; you want to eat better; time and busyness get in the way. If transforming your diet feels like more than you can take on right now, are there baby steps that would help you launch a manageable S Curve of gradual dietary improvement? Any positive change, however small, can be powerful (as we discussed in the Explorer chapter, little actions compound over time, resulting in big change) and can create space in your habits for additional improvements. Can you add one fresh fruit or vegetable to your day? Start somewhere.

You can also sleep your way to smart. "Focusing attention on learning something, followed by sleep, is a magic combination allowing for new synaptic connections," says researcher Barbara Oakley, author of the hit book and online course *Learning How to Learn*, and a collaborator with Terry Sejnowski (who you met in Accelerator, chapter 3).[9] Neurons activated while we are awake are reactivated during subsequent sleep. That's why you review your action board before going to bed. You are priming your brain to grow while you are sleeping.

Don't forget exercise, essential to metamorphosis. An experiment conducted by Sejnowski and his Salk Institute colleagues compared groups of mice that were active with groups that were kept inactive.[10] In both the active and the inactive groups, the rate at which new neurons were born was the same. But the mice that were active learned faster and retained more. Their synaptic networks increased at a faster rate, and the synapses were stronger. "Long-term potentiation," Sejnowski told me, "is enhanced by exercise."[11]

Say No to Yes

"Yes" lifted us off the launch point. The more we said yes, the more opportunities became available to us. But saying yes too often siphons momentum. We need to learn to say no to yes. During the final week of writing before this book's manuscript was due, for example, I didn't hem and haw and feel angst like I often do when I am asked for something. Pretty much, no matter what the ask, the answer was no. Being clear on the pressing priority, the pain that I often feel when I say no was alleviated. Saying no without nagging regret is essential for all of us if we are going to focus and transform.

Ryan Westwood understands this. His first foray into business was at age eleven.[12] Inspired by an English class assignment on "Why I want to be an entrepreneur," Westwood put price tags on all his beloved baseball and basketball cards, got the owner of a local shop to let him set up a kiosk in his store, and sold his sports cards, earning about $10. It felt like "magic," he says. By age forty, he'd built and sold two companies. When I interviewed Westwood for our podcast, he told me he had, over the course of his career, reached out to thousands of entrepreneurs to learn what made them successful. His conversation with Eric Morgan, then CEO of Workfront, stood out. Morgan told Westwood, "Once we found our differentiator, we focused, and we said, 'No.'"[13]

Westwood followed Morgan's advice. In his second business, Simplus, he transformed it from a "broad Salesforce implementer," to one in which "we only implement one Salesforce technology. We said no to everything else. It took incredible discipline and is counterintuitive to an entrepreneur. But by focusing and differentiating, we landed contracts with the biggest companies in the world."

As a from-the-cradle entrepreneur, Westwood tends to see S Curve opportunities everywhere. But being a smart growth leader, he knew that to grow Simplus, he would need to transform himself first. From a career standpoint, he said, "I started pursuing [only things] related to Simplus. Anything related to my book, anything related to a podcast, anything related to anything that did not promote Simplus, I said no to it."[14] Simplus employees followed his lead. They also narrowed their focus, made sacrifices, and kept their efforts concentrated rather than diluted. Westwood hung a sign in his office that read "Simplus." During meetings he would repeatedly point to it and say, "The main thing is the main thing." Through intense focus, supported by uncounted "nos," Westwood became a smart growth aficionado. After five years, Simplus sold for $250 million to Infosys. This success was not just a victory for Westwood; it transformed the lives of many of his employees. The company sale made it possible for families to buy homes and realize other dreams.

This kind of focus is a hallmark of the Metamorph. Transformation isn't achieved if we repeatedly interrupt the process in the sweet spot. If we can't focus and say no to new things, we risk becoming what George Leonard, author of the classic *Mastery*, labeled a "dabbler," who "might think of himself as an adventurer, a connoisseur of novelty, but he's probably closer to being what Carl Jung calls the *puer aeternus*, the eternal kid." Constantly saying yes to novelty is also saying no to mastery and bidding the Metamorph opportunity goodbye.

The challenge with all this naysaying is that we say yes for good reasons. Yes facilitates relationships. It's an essential word in a healthy ecosystem. But so is no, even though it's hard to say. If you see yourself as a helper by nature, or expect yourself to say yes, then saying no is going to cost you emotionally. Or if others expect you to say yes, then the cost of saying no will be accepting that you disappoint other people, often people whose approval matters to you, or people whose approval you need, like a boss, an influential friend, or a future opportunity. Learning to say no can involve painful identity adjustments.

Perhaps that's why I'm fascinated by the myth of Psyche, Greek goddess of the soul. Psyche's heroic journey illustrates the trials and triumphs of metamorphosis. Psyche was born a mortal woman. After becoming separated from her husband, the god Eros, Psyche is given four tasks by Eros's mother, Aphrodite. If Psyche successfully completes these tasks, she and Eros will be reunited. Initially Psyche is overcome with fear. She feels inadequate to accomplish any, much less all, of her tasks. But her cause is great. Psyche proceeds.

For the final task, Aphrodite directs Psyche to journey through the underworld, a fearsome and hazardous place, and fill a box with beauty ointment. Psyche is warned that she will encounter people who will beg for help and try to distract her. Psyche must say no if she hopes to accomplish her mission. Psyche triumphs. Psyche and Eros are reunited, and Eros spirits Psyche away to Mount Olympus, where she is made a goddess. If saying yes is to be anything more than mere obligation, we must say yes to what matters most to us (our values and *why*) and learn to say no to that which matters less. Learning to say no is part of maturing as a human being. Everyone will do it differently. But smart growth requires that everyone learn how to do it.

We need to stay focused if we are going to fly.

Pursue Optimized Tension

In the classic book *The Courage to Create*, Rollo May relates the story of a conference called "The Sky's the Limit" in which luminaries from wide-ranging fields would explore "human possibilities."

It turned out to be a dull affair. Many praises were sung to humanity's future, but as for humanity's present, no one would make specific commitments—financial commitments least of all. No one could agree on any new initiatives. When the conference finally broke up (to the relief of many), nothing substantive had been accomplished.[15]

"The sky's the limit" has a catchy ring, but down-to-earth parameters are what you need to grow. A little friction helps promote movement. It would be better said as, "The Sky's the Limit, but Gravity Is Good Too." "The creative act arises out of the struggle of human beings with and against that which limits them," May writes.[16]

To gain and maintain momentum in our transformation, what we need, and what characterizes the S Curve sweet spot for Metamorphs, is optimized tension. Of course, we are working to optimize tension at all points along the curve—if it's too hard, it needs to be made easier, or if it's too easy, it needs to be made harder, for example—but in the sweet spot, there is equilibrium. We have enough resources, but they aren't so abundant that we don't need to be resourceful—creative, innovative, persistent. We have enough expertise and capacity to make rapid progress, but not so much experience that we're bored, disengaged from learning, and no longer growing. Staying in the sweet spot, fully capturing opportunity, means constantly focusing on balancing the forces that can make our curve too challenging, with those that make it too easy.

This includes experiencing enough stress, but not too much.[17] Amy Arnsten, a neurobiologist researcher at Yale, has determined that you get the optimal level of stress, referred to as eustress, when you have the right level of two neurochemicals in your brain—dopamine and norepinephrine.[18] If levels are too low, there are no signals being transmitted, no communication between neurons. If levels are too high, the system crashes. At optimal levels, there is enough novelty that our neurons have something to talk about, but not so much that we trip the circuit.

There is value in every part of the S Curve. We can build momentum regardless of where we are. But obviously, we want to be in the sweet spot, accelerating into transformation as frequently as possible, for as long as possible, because that's where we are going to do our best work To do that we need to find that just-right level of stress.

But let's be realistic: change can hurt. Though we crave growth, novelty, and freedom to roam, we also crave wish fulfillment. The effort and persistence required for smart growth do not always, or even often, come naturally to us. English Irish poet and philosopher David Whyte wryly observes that "one of the astonishing qualities of being human is the measure of our reluctance to be here, actually." Whyte means all the ways you *don't* want to be here as regards your work or your relationships, all the ways you *don't* want to be here as a parent, as a leader. After all, adulting is tough.

Blaming yourself for your human nature, however, gets you nowhere. Whyte says, "I think self-compassion has to do with the ability to understand and even to cultivate a sense of humor about all the ways you just don't want to be here. To embody your reluctance and . . . once it's embodied, to allow it to actually start to change into something else."[19] This is metamorphosis. First, acknowledge your aversion, not necessarily to change itself, but to the hard work change demands. Second, start changing.

My second-great-grandfather, Ebenezer Bryce, was a nineteenth-century shipbuilder and immigrant from Scotland. He came to the United States as a young man in 1854, married Mary Park in Salt Lake City, Utah, and raised a large family. A few years into their marriage, Ebenezer was asked to build a chapel in a remote valley. This was building, his vocation, but not of ships, and became a moment of optimized tension—the successful leveraging of the old and new, the familiar and unknown.

The Pine Valley Chapel that Ebenezer built is still in use today, listed on the National Register of Historic Places, and, remarkably, constructed like an upside-down ship. The chapel roof looks like a conventional roof, but the substructure is shaped like a ship's hull. Ebenezer Bryce was a pioneer innovator and a disruptor.

With that challenge conquered, Ebenezer and his family next went homesteading in what is now Bryce Canyon National Park (named for him) in Utah, an otherworldly landscape of red-rock geological splendor, and as Ebenezer put it, "a hell of a place to lose a cow."[20] Bryce Canyon was a far cry from Glasgow—in Glasgow, it rains. Undeterred, Ebenezer and Mary innovated, leveraging their old skills to maximize new resources. They grew, adapted, and made a wilderness blossom.

The Bryces would eventually establish the eponymous community in Arizona where they finished out their inspiring lives. To me, Ebenezer's golden years embody the joy of metamorphosis. My ancestor was fully transformed, from a young Scottish shipbuilder to a seasoned American pioneer.

Once a caterpillar, now a butterfly.

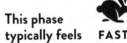

Metamorph Takeaways

This phase typically feels　**FAST**

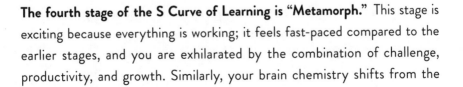

The fourth stage of the S Curve of Learning is "Metamorph." This stage is exciting because everything is working; it feels fast-paced compared to the earlier stages, and you are exhilarated by the combination of challenge, productivity, and growth. Similarly, your brain chemistry shifts from the headwinds of stress response to providing supportive dopamine rewards as your predictive model improves. This Metamorph phase of growth involves a shift in identity; the S Curve moves from being something you *do* (for example, "I exercise by running") to increasingly becoming something you *are* (for example, "I'm a runner.")

This stage in your smart growth requires focus and a concentration of energy. As a Metamorph, momentum is strong and there is still considerable room for growth. The fact that everything is working well presents a paradoxical challenge. You may feel you are done; you may feel like jumping to a new S Curve, but now is the time to focus and concentrate your energy on the task at hand, so you understand your growth and shape it. The better your grasp of how growth is achieved, the greater your capacity to affect it. Here are five lenses to help sustain your focus—techniques to concentrate your energies so you can maintain momentum:

- **Focus lens 1—Stay in the moment.** You have the resources available, and the competence to utilize them, but success requires staying focused on the present moment, and being deliberate about what you focus on. You can consciously help accelerate your growth when you give your attention to the right things. Focus, so you can fly.

- **Focus lens 2—Triumph over your triggers.** The pain or loss that you have experienced—especially in childhood—can be easily triggered and derail your focus. These emotional triggers can sap your confidence and leave you vulnerable to discouragement in ways that can slow the momentum of your growth. Pretending you don't have triggers only increases their destructive power. But you can triumph over them. Successful people consciously know their triggers and have plans to minimize or work around them, and find healing and acceptance in meaningful ways.

- **Focus lens 3—Healthy body, sharp mind.** Maintaining focus through the excitement and distractions of this phase requires a sharp mind. Your body is the best whetstone to sharpen your mind, so what you eat, how you sleep, and how often you exercise all have a significant contribution to your focus. A healthy body helps your brain be its best self.

- **Focus lens 4—Say no to yes.** The faster pace and exciting results of this stage will open doors to more opportunities. But increased opportunity can also increase the distraction from your main purpose. The few new opportunities to consider are those that directly contribute toward the goals of this S Curve. All others become a diversion that will slow the hard-won momentum you've started to experience. The Metamorph says no to distractions and yes to accelerating momentum on the S Curve.

- **Focus lens 5—Pursue optimized tension.** While you may fantasize about days free of any tension, your growth is maximized in conditions of optimized tension—you have enough resources, but not so many that you don't need to be resourceful, creative, innovative, and persistent. You have enough expertise and capacity to make rapid progress, but not so much that you're bored, disengaged from learning, and no longer growing. This is the good kind of stress: high levels of novelty but not enough to trip a circuit.

Make the most of the sweet spot for as long as possible, because that's where you are going to do your best work. This is where the magic happens, where caterpillars become butterflies.

Sweet Spot Summary for Smart Growth Leaders

The sweet spot of the S Curve feels *fast* because it is fast. Growth is apparent. People at this stage are transitioning from doing to being. Depending on the personality type, confidence tends to strengthen, and overconfidence tends to dissipate as experience deepens. The sweet spot is exhilarating, with stress at optimal levels. There's the right balance of familiar information and tasks, with the brain's predictive model becoming increasingly accurate. The difficult questions around identity have faded. Potential is being realized, but opportunities remain.

The hallmarks of the sweet spot are outlined in the following Goldilocks Table. Right now, the chair is not too small, and it's not too big, it's just right. Once you as a leader understand the experiences and emotions of your sweet spotters, you can create an ecosystem where they can be successful during this phase of their growth.

GOLDILOCKS TABLE

Plotting the Emotional Journey of Growth

Dimensions	Launch Point: Slow	Sweet Spot: Fast
Confidence	The feeling of confidence is seldom aligned to reality at the launch. Some personalities will feel no confidence in this new area and fight imposter syndrome and insecurities that drain their energy. Other personalities will feel more confident than their limited experience warrants, leading to costly and avoidable mistakes.	As you gain experience, the overconfidence or imposter syndrome (depending on personality) tends to fade and confidence strengthens.
Identity	Difficult and deep questions emerge: • I'm not good at this. Do I have value? • Is doing something like this aligned with who I am . . . or even want to be?	The difficult questions have faded: "I'm good at this!" . . . but it's not an established part of your identity yet.
Familiarity	Much about this area is brand new, like exploring a new country. Past experience in other areas can provide valuable orientation but should be treated cautiously so you don't miss the important details and differences.	This area is mostly familiar but still has some newness and novelty.
Mental state	Some personalities find this stressful, feeling overwhelmed by the volume of new information to process and things to learn. Other personalities find all the new stimuli exhilarating. Both need to keep these tendencies from pulling them off the path of deliberate growth.	You have just the right balance of familiar information or tasks and new challenges. In many cases, the experience is one of flow state where you are fully immersed and have an enjoyable feeling of energized focus and full involvement.
Value proposition	Considerable untapped potential waits on the other side of the investment. Uncertainties remain, but the reward seems worth it.	You are actively realizing much of the potential, and additional opportunities remain. Uncertainty is considerably lessened because of the momentum you've built in this stage.
Successful mindset	Success at this stage flows from leaning into the challenge—saying yes and experimenting with new approaches, ways of being, and relationships.	You shift from always saying yes and broad experimentation to learning to say no so that you can focus and execute.
Support network	A supportive network may be available, but you generally don't know who is in the network or how to access them . . . even if you did, you're not sure you'd want to because you don't want to look needy.	You know who to ask for help, when to ask, and how to best leverage help; you are comfortable asking for help.

Dimensions	Launch Point: Slow	Sweet Spot: Fast
Decision approach	The tendency for most is to directly follow the procedure and guidance of authority figures.	You are able to recognize levels of uncertainty in authority figures and different situations and contexts.
Knowledge base	You are starting to learn important facts and the needed language . . . but not enough to be efficient or effective. You can think you know more than you do because you don't know what you don't know.	You know how to be efficient and effective. You increasingly know what you don't know.
Energy and output	For most, this new challenge takes more energy than you expected, and the progress is slower than expected.	You can get more done with less energy than ever; the momentum is exhilarating and there is no end in sight.

Grow Your People: Managing People in the Sweet Spot

Based on our data, people in the sweet spot are generally very comfortable in their work performance and believe they are excelling. They are capable of asking questions that lead to innovation and growth, and they also have the internal resources and network of relationships needed to put ideas into action. Highly competent, they are the go-to people on your team. They are experiencing flow. Help them stay in flow by coaching them on what to prioritize.

Sweet spotters are accelerating in part because of your focus on their growth. You are ensuring they are adequately resourced, have sufficient responsibility and accountability, and are connected to the team's vision, to team members, and especially to you. Because they feel valued and appreciated, and know you are focused on their personal growth and development, they tackle challenges with gusto. (For more on how to create an environment that fosters growth, see Ecosystem, chapter 7.)

It's easy to ignore those who are producing well and take them for granted. Proactively encourage them to lift their heads occasionally to see where they're going and what the pinnacle of the S looks like. Have conversations about the potential next S Curve. Key to retaining these high performers is not only helping them focus, but staying focused on their perception of where they are in their growth.

Below is a summary table of how to manage people in the sweet spot based on both the career stage of the individual and the type of organization in which you work.

HOW TO MANAGE PEOPLE AT THE SWEET SPOT

Leading at Sweet Spot Theme: FOCUS

	TYPE OF ORGANIZATION		
	Young and/or growing	Advancing and/or midstage	Historic and/or complex
Early career	As individuals accelerate into the sweet spot, underscore the value they are creating, especially in the absence of concrete career paths. Help people see what they are a part of and what is possible for the future. Let them understand and be a part of the vision for what is being built. They are hungry to know that what they do matters. Focus on them. See them. Ensure that there is the right blend between disciplined feedback and frequent verbal praise for concrete wins. The momentum of the company can lead to personal acceleration and metamorphosis.	With a healthy pipeline and structure in place, work to ensure that paths for growth and development are identified and viable. For continued acceleration, provide stretch assignments individually, but also collectively. Continue with career path conversations to align with their needs and yours, building loyalty, engagement, and contribution.	Movement within larger organizations tends to be easier from a structural standpoint, but highly driven sweet spotters can hit obstacles when it comes to process. There can also be the challenge of getting lost in the mix. Is how you track progress aligned with how you want to grow your people? Be deliberate about listening to people's challenges and look for opportunities to advocate and change what is within your span of control.

	TYPE OF ORGANIZATION		
	Young and/or growing	**Advancing and/or midstage**	**Historic and/or complex**
Midcareer	Creating impact and doing it readily is something that midcareer sweet spotters can take for granted. As a leader, it is critical you are prepared to support them in this acceleration phase but also to remind them that metamorphosis involves patience. As your business grows, so do the opportunities for this group. Think intentionally about growth plans not only for them, but as they move into mastery and consider the next growth cycle.	Even if people don't know what the next S Curve will look like, growth at this stage is palpable. Keep it fun by unleashing their considerable technical skills on stretch projects. Leverage this windfall of goodwill and engagement by encouraging people to partner and collaborate across the organization.	There are often mobility opportunities for people early in their career. Make sure that mid- and expert levels are also encouraged and supported in moving internally. Create systems that allow for lateral and vertical shifts at all ages and stages within the company. Team culture is critical for retaining top talent. As a leader of a business unit, create an ecosystem where people believe they can grow.
Expert career	Seeking out sweet spot opportunities is a deliberate choice. People at the expert level have often sacrificed more-lucrative opportunities for trying their hand at a new challenge. If you are attracting experts, yours is likely a culture that is itself in the sweet spot.	Experts are making the choice to work with you because they believe they can continue to grow. Give them that opportunity. Remember to focus on and appreciate them.	Further promotions may not be an option, but that doesn't mean they can't be growing—and quickly. Consider these individuals for matrix teams, mentors, and culture hosts. Avoid the misperception that technical competence equates to leadership ability.

Additional Tips for Managers

- Sweet spotters are going fast. They are performing well. But even the fastest driver needs a pit crew. Help them drive their CAR—ensure that they feel competent, autonomous, and related.

- **Competence.** The sweet spot is the place of optimized constraints. Some of the natural constraints have dissolved. But just as a car can't drive on ice, people can't move up the S Curve without some friction. Allow people on your team to struggle; constraints are tools of creation. Stretch assignments are how an Accelerator becomes a Metamorph.

- **Autonomy.** Provide resources and then allow your people to self-govern. As managers (and parents), we often flip-flop between giving too much freedom and not enough. Too much freedom comes when we delegate too much—providing little guidance or feedback, and insufficient resources. Too little freedom is micro-managing. If you are micromanaging, is it because individuals aren't yet competent, or because you don't want to delegate? We tend to delegate work we need to do (because it's hard) and hang on to the work we shouldn't—the top of the S Curve stuff that soothes our insecure self. In the sweet spot, people are competent. If you don't allow them the latitude to execute, you stunt their growth—and yours. Autonomy is also the freedom to say no. As you encourage your people to focus and prioritize, are you allowing, encouraging, and requiring them to say no, including to you?

- **Relatedness.** Because things are going well, it's easy to start taking people for granted. I had a coaching client tell me that one of his sweet spotters was leaving because he didn't know if his boss thought he was doing a good job. Acknowledge good work by delivering concrete feedback about what *is* working and what you and the team are learning because of and from the individual.

• The best way to help your team achieve confidence—to drive their CAR—is to listen to what they have to say. When you listen while people voice their ideas, they are teaching themselves and developing competence. When you listen, and your colleague feels heard, they will have the real-time experience of affecting the outcome, and they will feel that they belong and matter. Listening is magic.

- When your sweet spotters reach out, be available. When you have one-on-ones scheduled, keep those appointments. You may feel like you don't have time, and things are working, so you don't need to make time. However, if you cancel, you will have likely canceled the meeting they most anticipated and felt they needed that week.

- Establish a practice that reminds your team to work together. At the beginning of most of our team meetings, we say aloud Alan Mulally's *Working Together* principles so that we are all psychologically sitting on the same side of the table. These are twelve guiding principles articulated by visionary CEO Alan Mulally to deliver the Boeing 777 on time and on budget, and later to execute a turnaround as chief executive of the Ford Motor Company.[1] Reinforce working together by calling out when people do cooperate (for example, "This project was successful in part because of how the two of you collaborated").

- Beware your ego. As your sweet spotters get the work done, they increase their confidence and utilize the resources available to them, including your support. In this situation, there is the risk that you could feel like they are using up *your* resources, driving their car in *your* lane. Make sure there's enough gas in your tank so you can emotionally fuel both your team's growth and your own.

- When you are going fast, you may fear that you will revert to your mean. Remind your organization that momentum builds momentum. What you do today affects tomorrow, so invest the knowledge and resources you have today toward a stronger future. That is smart growth.

Grow Your Company: Sweet Spot Implications for Leaders

Following are concrete ways to apply the S Curve of Learning model and the S Curve Insight Platform to grow your organization.[2]

- To achieve peak performance as a team, a strong majority (that is, at least 60 percent) of your team should be in the sweet spot. Team members in this stage are able to build and sustain the momentum of accomplishments, getting the critical work done on time, on budget, day after day. Crucial though they are, they shouldn't be 100 percent of your team. You also need fresh perspectives and energy from those on the launch point to fuel innovation and the wisdom of those in mastery to provide mentoring and guidance on difficult judgment calls.

- If the majority of your team is in the sweet spot, it's humming along. Your team members are competent in their contribution and feel connected to one another and the overall mission of the company. They can draw on the experience of those in mastery (plus their own expertise) while shouldering the additional work that comes with helping those on the launch point become increasingly effective. Because everything is working, you may be tempted to relax, but you should watch for the possibility that your team can gradually, then suddenly, become slightly bored. Now is the time to develop a plan before a large contingent of your team reaches the top of their respective S Curves.

- Monitor and codify best practices so they can be replicated across the organization.

PART THREE

MASTERY

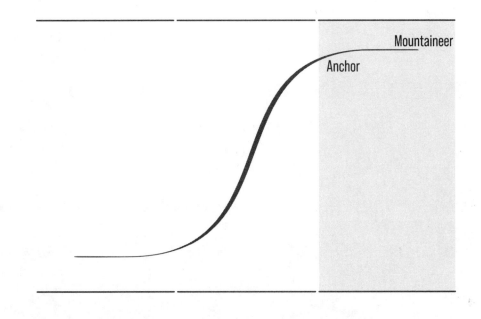

5 Anchor

I used to be so delusional. I always imagined I could be more
than I was, and eventually I grew into that person.

—LADY GAGA

Erik Orton said he was "treading water" working on Broadway as a theater producer. To make ends meet when one of his shows closed abruptly,
he picked up some gigs doing graphic design. One night after work, Orton
walked past marinas along the Hudson River where small yachts and sail-
boats were moored. Seeing their lights mirrored on the water's black surface captured Orton's imagination. He wanted to learn how to sail.[1]

His wife, Emily, encouraged him. They and their two oldest daughters
started taking weekly lessons. The Orton family started to, literally, learn
the ropes. They joined a sailing club.

It would have been hard for Orton to imagine when he glimpsed the
twinkling lights on the water that eventually he and his entire family—wife,
five children with an age range of six to sixteen, the youngest born with
Down syndrome—would push pause on their life in Manhattan for a year,
to live on a boat and sail the Atlantic.

But they did. After five years of practice, all seven Ortons headed
to the Caribbean. There, they bought a second-hand catamaran, the

thirty-eight-foot *Fezywig*, moored on the island of St. Martin, in the Netherland Antilles.[2]

Sometimes S Curves of Learning lead you to strange waters. Not every S Curve is work and career oriented. Sometimes you want to pursue big growth outside the workplace.

The *Fezywig* wasn't spacious: with four small cabins and two bathrooms below deck, it was smaller than their two-bedroom New York apartment. Still, after harboring in place for several months, making repairs and discovering, as Orton described it to me, "a steep learning curve of realizing how much we did not know and how in over our heads we were," the Ortons cast off the lines and set sail.

The Orton's ultimate destination was New York City. After several short trips in and around St. Kitts and Antigua, *Fezywig* got her last tune-up back in St. Martin, and the Ortons began to sail north, through the Virgin Islands, past Puerto Rico, past the Bahamas. They sailed west to Florida and then into colder waters: up the Atlantic seaboard. The Carolinas slipped past. Then the Chesapeake, then the Jersey Shore.

Six years and more than two thousand nautical miles since their first sailing lesson, the Hudson River and the bright lights of Midtown came into view. Having sailed from the Dutch Caribbean to the Statue of Liberty, the Ortons docked their faithful *Fezywig* and walked home. Home through the familiar, noisy streets to the same apartment they left when they went to sea. Through many adventures, the Ortons learned to work with the open sea, and with one another.

It wasn't always smooth sailing. Erik discovered he could get seasick. Emily wasn't a fan of deep water. Rinsing the kids' laundry in a bucket and having to make their own fresh water was not modern convenience. "Sailing was not my idea," Emily told me, "but it became my dream." Sometimes it was terrifying. Sometimes it was thrilling. Sometimes it was tedious. "It was a struggle," Emily says. "But I'm all about learning." Emily understands smart growth; she and Erik are smart growth leaders of their family. They grow, they help their children grow, the family grows.

Through these voyages, the Ortons reached the top of their S Curve of Learning, transforming from a couple who wanted to learn to sail into sailors. Sailing was no longer a skill they were working to develop or a dream they wanted to fulfill. It was—and is—what they are. They wrote a bestselling book, *Seven at Sea: Why a New York City Family Cast Off Convention for a Life-Changing Year on a Sailboat*. The S Curve they set out to conquer—to learn how to sail and do it as a family—has been vanquished. "This can't be undone," Emily says. "This is now ours."

They had reached, appropriately enough, the Anchor phase of the S Curve. You aren't an anchor or an anchorer, but your new behavior is anchored and now so much a part of you that you would have to jump to a new learning curve to make additional meaningful change. Once you have anchored new knowledge or skills, they are trusted. You trust your own abilities. You trust the abilities of your people and your organization: shipmates in the same boat. And you trust that what you accomplished has lasting merit, that it was worthwhile. The Anchor stage is a brief season of rest and reflection before you take the next leap. Perseverance (and blisters) got the Ortons to the sweet spot, relatedness and teamwork got them to safe harbor, and trust was part of the reward. Erik says, "The size of your dreams is in proportion to how much you trust yourself."

At the high end of the S Curve, we are in mastery. Ease displaces effort. Our newly learned skills and behavior are anchored in us, and what was novel and difficult has become nearly effortless and automatic. The voyage is over. The Anchor phase is marked by the stability and confidence we have established, and declining momentum as we glide into the harbor. We have achieved what we hoped to accomplish, but our potential for additional growth on this curve is greatly diminished and further progress is slow. Slow, fast, slow—that is how we grow.

Erik Orton said he was treading water because he had been demoralized, feeling like a failure after an important career opportunity unexpectedly sank. In contrast, being at anchor is accompanied by a sense of achievement. Now is a time to pause and reflect, appreciate the accomplishment.

Mission Accomplished

Let's recap. We started with an opportunity, or opportunities, and explored the potential of one or more S Curves of Learning with our seven-question template (see Explorer, chapter 1). Our objective? To determine if the option we're most attracted to (or that we've been forced to accept for the time being) could produce smart growth that will exceed the price we pay to pursue it. We calculated. Is it achievable, easy to test, familiar, yet novel? While much of the cost was qualitative—how much will I need to change to be who I aspire to be—some of the cost can be quantified, the financial investment required or the time commitment involved.

For Emily and Erik Orton, this required considering the cost of a sailboat, repairs, living at sea, the impact of time away from Erik's conventional career. They are not wealthy. Emily was a stay-at-home, homeschooling mom. But the Ortons wanted to have a life-changing experience with their children. Here's a peek into their dialogue about the financial cost:

> *Emily:* What's the worst that could happen?
>
> *Erik:* We could be financially ruined, never recover, have to send our kids to live with relatives, and all our friends will think we're idiots.

"We agreed it wasn't likely," Emily said, "and we'd still be young enough to make a comeback if it happened." In terms of fulfillment of purpose, personal and family growth, and ensuing opportunities, the costs were subsumed by the potential reward.[3] The Ortons acted.

If the results of your own exploration and collection are positive, and you are willing to commit and persevere, you can hopefully power through the painful obstacles of the launch point into the sweet spot. Ever smart about your growth, you'll then stay focused until your metamorphosis is complete.

Recalling his family's penultimate day aboard *Fezywig*, Erik Orton wrote:

> We sailed past the basin where we had first learned to sail. I couldn't help but laugh at our first, chaotic family sail there. We had bounced off channel pylons, dropped sail ties into the water, and generally bumbled around while Eli and Lilly (our two youngest children) screamed their heads off. We still had

our issues, but now we more or less had our act together. That first sail felt like another life. I was a different person now. So was Emily. We all were.

Allow yourself to celebrate in the Anchor phase. Becoming the different people that we set out to be is cause for it. Social anthropologist Frank E. Manning writes, "Celebration is an important part of our cultural repertoire—it's the means through which people claim their identity and fashion their sense of purpose."[4] Celebration draws a symbolic line between old and new, giving us a clearer sense of how far we've come.

Remember how former Baxter CEO Harry Kraemer (from the introduction) came to Anchor after a storied business career.[5] But he didn't take much of a break before he set a course for the uncharted waters of academia. Did Kraemer get a chance to celebrate, I wondered?

He told me he did, and in a remarkable way. He had six weeks free before he started teaching at Kellogg School of Management. What might his wife, Julie Kraemer, have in mind? "She said, 'That's easy.' We're going to fly to Europe with the five kids—all bizarre ages." Kraemer children ranged from three to sixteen. And they weren't going to an all-inclusive resort either. All seven Kraemers flew to Paris and rented a van. "Remember that movie *Family Vacation* with Chevy Chase?" Kraemer said. No travel itinerary. No hotel reservations. "Wherever we end up, we end up."

Four weeks later, the Kraemers ended up in Rome. More than a mere road trip, this was a celebration, a trek, and a family bonding experience—an important bookend to Kraemer's corporate career.

A Cause for Celebration

B. J. Fogg advocates celebration to mark what I would call the Anchor point on even the smallest of S Curves. Fogg is a leading behavioral scientist: founder-director of the Behavior Design Lab at Stanford University. Fogg's work explores the causal relationship between emotions and habits. Feelings come first, Fogg teaches. Based on extensive research and the real-time coaching of over forty thousand people, Fogg's theory posits that habit formation is not, as the popular formula teaches, a matter of twenty-one days of consistent practice.[6] With pleasure and positive emotions being part of the brain's reward system, celebrating our achievements anchors that emotional uplift in our memory. "Emotions create habits," he says.

Fogg recommends we celebrate at three points that map well to the S Curve. Identify a new skill or behavior you are developing. Celebrate when you remember to perform it (launch point), celebrate while you're performing it (sweet spot), celebrate when you finish performing it (mastery). Celebration can be as simple as looking at yourself in the mirror and saying, "Victory." The positive feelings generated by celebration help our brains internalize a new habit.

Sometimes, particularly when we're tired, it's easy to forget what we did well, what we accomplished in our most recent waking hours. Self-criticism can convince us the day was a failure, a waste. Remember to applaud the little victories. This is yet another good reason to journal.

Celebrating a Willingness to Fail

What constitutes a victory, or amounts to a defeat, is often a matter of perspective. If Sifan Hassan—2019 women's world champion runner—were to run a 10K in thirty-five minutes, she would probably call it a defeat. If I were to run a 10K in seventy-five minutes, I'd call that a victory. Keep in mind that every expert was once a neophyte, making childlike mistakes, dropping sail lines into the water or getting seasick, tackling something wholly unfamiliar. When you have the courage to take on a new challenge, to get in over your head, the courage you evince is a victory itself. It is cause for celebration, regardless of the specific outcome. A lot of smart growth is fueled by failure turned to good purpose. Failure isn't failure if it gives you power to progress.

That's what Glen Nelson learned when he was brave enough to pick up a sketch pad. Nelson is a nonfiction writer and art curator by profession. As cofounder and codirector of the nonprofit Center for Latter-day Saint Arts in New York City, Nelson celebrates the work of other Latter-day Saint artists and serves as a hub for their creative community.[7] Painters, actors, writers, choreographers, composers, musicians, playwrights—these LDS creators have been drawn to New York for over a century. Their shared culture and faith make them a unique part of New York City's varied art scene.

The concept behind the center came to Nelson in the late nineties. Nelson was a recent New York University graduate working as an opera librettist around the time a young composer—a student at the Juilliard School—approached him with a simple question.[8] Nelson said, "She was programming her master's degree recital and wanted to perform at least one work by a composer who shared her beliefs. 'Where can I go,' she asked, 'to find music that expresses my belief?' The short answer was, nowhere. It doesn't exist."

It occurred to Nelson that artists within his faith tradition needed such a place to gather expressions, preserve them, and celebrate both the artwork and the broader culture it reflects to anchor the culture's identity. If such an ecosystem did not exist to nurture and stimulate Latter-day Saint artists in New York, Nelson resolved to create one himself.

Two decades later, Nelson and his codirectors are still actively promoting works by LDS creators. In 2021 they inaugurated their first private gallery directly across from Juilliard and the Metropolitan Opera.

But before that they had to endure 2020 and the Covid-19 pandemic, which put their plans temporarily on hold. New York art galleries closed. Nelson was stuck on standby, stuck at home on the Upper West Side. So he launched a new learning curve, creating his own art. "I've wanted to try to draw for as long as I can remember," he told me, "but I've always psyched myself out."

Believing you can do something can be a challenge, especially when you're an adult. In Collector (chapter 2), we discussed how the flexible growth mindset of childhood starts to harden into fixed self-assumptions. Having first trained as a dancer, however, Nelson was accustomed to stretching.

Nelson purchased the venerable *Drawing on the Right Side of the Brain* by Betty Edwards. His goal was to read the book, complete its exercises, and journal about the experience. He shared some of his drawings via the blog *Can I Draw If I Think, "I Can't Draw"?* so it's easy to follow his progress.[9]

The project ended on April 2, 2020, less than two weeks after it began.

In the first two days, he describes himself as nervous, embarrassed, and skittish to display his obviously amateur efforts. He realizes that he's impatient and not a close observer, an idiosyncrasy that this learning curve requires him to confront. "I'm realizing immediately that to draw, I need to slow it down and get the parts of my brain involved that can measure the distances between one thing and another thing and then capture that on the page," he writes on the second day.

The next day, he's "starting to think of drawings I'd like to make in the future." In only three days, Nelson is beginning to think of himself as someone who draws, rather than as someone who doesn't even doodle. On day four, he completes the exercise and writes, "I felt like a real artist doing that." On this chronologically brief S Curve, I believe this marks his tip into the steep sweet spot. The next few days' exercises posed new challenges, but Nelson was able to apply techniques he had already learned and stretch himself to solve the problems those drawings presented. "Normally," he wrote, "I would have quit after trying and failing for a while."

Nearing the end of the workbook, he expresses dread about a portrait exercise; the first assignment had been a self-portrait, and the result hadn't pleased him, "The book warned me about these self-doubts and advised me to push through them." He did. Some parts still exceeded his ability to execute as he would have liked. "And yet, when I look back at the first self-portrait I made just a week ago, I know I've come a long way. I need to feel motivated and pleased by that." He concludes, "This has been transformational for me."

"Motivated and pleased" is that sense of quiet celebration at the Anchor stage, that moment where we commemorate the crossing from the old to the new. If we think of Nelson's S Curve as setting out to master all the nuances of drawing, then he's still on the launch point—collecting. But he gave this S Curve specific parameters: to read the book, complete the exercises, and journal. It was a brief, but challenging learning curve. It was a solid smart growth win. Whether your S Curve is modest or monumental, you *have* changed. In the aggregate, many small anchorings like this add up to major growth.

Etta King, with whom I volunteer in the Relief Society, a women's organization, shared a similar anchoring experience from a printmaking class.[10]

She was hesitant; she had taken a swipe at this art form in college but couldn't create with her hands what was in her head. At the end of the semester, she had turned in her tools and thought that was that. This is not uncommon when trying something new; it's why we explore and collect. Some S Curves are too financially, emotionally, or psychologically costly and frustrating to provide value, and it's good to figure that out early rather than late.

Twenty years later, notwithstanding demanding family and work responsibilities, King wanted to try again. A family friend and art professor, Doug Himes, suggested she audit his course at nearby Southern Virginia University. "I forgot how time consuming it was. Sometimes it took me more than an hour to clean up the ink and my workspace." She continues, "It was hard, so hard. On the final project (as with Nelson, a self-portrait), I wanted to give up. My tendency is, if it can't be perfect or the best, I'm not going to do it at all."

Himes provided the support all good leaders give, launch pointers. He was both an excellent instructor and a champion encourager. He continually said to King, "It's about the process, not the product. Try again. Adjust this. Try again."

Perfectionism is the enemy of smart growth for many of us. British writer and theologian G. K. Chesterton said, "Anything worth doing is worth doing badly." If we are to reach our potential, we need to be brave enough to be imperfect. When King bravely turned her focus to the process instead of the quality of the finished product, she produced an imperfect art piece, but there was also progress that had before eluded her, and a new sense of joy and freedom in the process. Celebrating her anchoring moment, King told me, "It was really good to know that I could do something hard, and that it didn't have to be perfect."

In their 2006 book, *Savoring: A New Model of Positive Experience*, positive psychology experts Fred B. Bryant and the late Joseph Veroff explain that the celebration of achievement is an internal experience as much as it is an external one.[11] This doesn't mean we don't commemorate the occasion with others, but much of the meaning associated with a meaningful ending is the meaning we alone make of it, the value we ultimately internalize from the hope, belief, and effort we've expended in reaching our objective.

Bryant's own story of summiting fourteen-thousand-foot Snowmass Mountain in the Colorado Rockies is a perfect example of anchoring celebration. Bryant had made two prior, unsuccessful attempts. He knew that reaching this pinnacle was probably a once-in-a-lifetime event. Finally at the summit, he lingered with his friends, taking in the spectacular view, and then embraced them and expressed his gratitude to be sharing his joy in the moment with them.

Internally, Bryant was reflecting. He remembered his first commitment to the quest. He thought about all the training, the prep work, the maps, the vagaries of weather, the back injury that almost thwarted him, and the gnawing fear he'd never make it. The adversity he'd encountered made the delayed realization of the dream more meaningful. He anticipated relating the experience to his family. He'd be proud to recall it in later years, and he imagined the pride his late grandfather, an avid outdoorsman, would have had in his accomplishment. Bryant took time to savor the sensations of the moment—the smell and taste of the cold, pine-scented air, the sound of the wind and how it felt on his face, the details of the view before him. He committed these meaning-making and meaning-internalizing specifics to memory. It was a quiet celebration, lasting just ten minutes. The weather was turning. Time to descend.

Staying present in the many moments—including the mundane ones—of an S Curve will bring you to the Anchor stage. When you arrive there, do yourself the honor of being present and taking time to recognize what you've accomplished. This is key to celebrating your achievement. It is key to capturing this fleeting, liminal space, where the past flows into the present, and the present promises all the future may hold. Pause to Anchor this victory in your memory.

Bittersweet Reflections

While anchoring is cause for celebration, it is not a time of unmitigated happiness. The satisfaction of reaching the harbor is also accompanied by sadness that the voyage has come to an end. It's important to acknowledge that poignancy—-there is celebration, gratitude, and a touch of sorrow.

We may also feel at loose ends, a little lost without the structure our learning curve required.

Dan Pink, author of multiple *New York Times*–bestselling books on business and human behavior, summarizes, "Adding a small component of sadness to an otherwise happy moment elevates the moment rather than diminishing it. The best endings don't leave us happy. They produce something richer. A rush of unexpected insight, a fleeting moment of transcendence."[12]

At the high end of the learning curve, the plants in the pond have proliferated across the surface; their roots have spread to fill the pond floor. There is a splendid spectacle of blossoms, but a whiff of decay as well. The flowers' blooming is fleeting. The lily pads cover the pond, preventing sunlight from penetrating the water and reaching the roots, the soil and its nutrients are depleted, the once abundant resources have been exhausted. In this particular pond, there is no more room for the lilies to grow. But those flowers! At this moment? How can we not pause to glory in them?

The Ortons' sailing adventure didn't wrap up quite as tidily as my initial recounting may have made it seem. They did dock in Manhattan, in the middle of the night, and walk home. But that was about three weeks after they planned to reach port. On what was meant to be their last night at sea, the Ortons encountered high winds and rough water. They sought shelter a bit south of their destination. While in port, they tore a hole in the bottom of their boat. They were taking on water at a brisk pace. Bailing frantically, they saved the boat and had it hauled out of the water for repairs. They had to leave *Fezywig* and rent an SUV to get seven weary sailors home. Orton writes in *Seven at Sea*, "We drove up I-95 and across the George Washington Bridge, turned onto Broadway, and pulled into a parking space across the street from our apartment building. We sat in the car in silence. Karina offered a prayer for all of us. Then she cried. Emily cried, silent tears running down her face."

Returning to *Fezywig* to unload and clean her, Orton says, "We needed to see if she was okay. We needed to remind each other we were okay. We patted her hull and took a few pictures. Good boat. We walked to the dock with all the kids and noticed the sunset." When the repairs were complete, the family sailed the boat up the Hudson. They took pictures that didn't turn out well in the fading light. "We would have to remember this one in our minds," writes Orton. "Emily and the kids turned on music and danced on deck. This was definitely something worth celebrating." They tied up and *then* walked home.

Zaza Pachulia (Accelerator, chapter 3) had reached the pinnacle of his sport and the top of his S Curve as a member of the 2017 and 2018 world champion Golden State Warriors. After poignant reflection, he decided to celebrate the achievement by retiring. "I wish I could play basketball the rest of my life," he told me, "but it's just not possible." Meanwhile, he had four children, ranging in age from twelve to three. He'd been playing since before they were born. He could now spend more time with his family. Pachulia was "thankful, great career, sixteen years in the game. This game gave me a lot."[13] He was anchored.

It helped that he had a job offer in management from the Golden State Warriors. They offered various leadership positions. All sounded interesting. He said, "How about I do everything?" So, Pachulia's first year after retiring as a player, the challenging pandemic season of 2019–2020, that's what he did. He has determined that he doesn't want to coach, but the exploration and data collection continue on the business side. Consistently smart about his growth, he will likely scale multiple operational S Curves before he leaves professional basketball—if he ever does.

Milestones of Gratitude and Grief

As I conduct interviews for the *Disrupt Yourself* podcast, I'm continually reminded that many of the high-achieving people I talk to are immigrants (like Zaza Pachulia) or the children of immigrants (Erik Orton is a second-generation American). For centuries, immigrants have left their homelands under duress, escaping the consequences of war, famine, or a lack of economic opportunity.[14]

Anchoring in a new land marks the end of a journey. In that moment, immigrants experience perhaps this poignant mix of celebration and sorrow as strongly or more strongly than anyone. Angela Blanchard, the globally prominent expert practitioner in community development who you met in Explorer (chapter 1), has worked with refugees and immigrants for most of her life. "At every milestone," she says, "there will be gratitude and grief in equal measure."

I'm a descendant of immigrants to the United States. Some of my ancestors on my mother's side were Lowland Scots, such as Ebenezer Bryce. On my father's side, I'm part Cornish, descended from headstrong Celtic people who long ago were pushed into the rugged extremity of England's southwest.

My Cornish ancestors left their homes as an exploding population exhausted local resources. In the nineteenth century, Cornwall, long a center of copper mining, was also a world leader in the technologies required to prevent flooding, create ventilation, and manage other mine hazards, along with the day-to-day necessities of getting ore mined hundreds of feet below ground up to the surface.[15]

Though Cornwall's mines were depleted, demand for copper was skyrocketing abroad. Opportunity abounded for technicians who would cross seas. Twenty percent or more of the Cornish population emigrated each decade during the late 1800s. They migrated to the United States, of course, but also to Australia, South Africa, Mexico, and elsewhere.

With them, they brought the mining technology, but also Methodist chapels and distinctive cemeteries.[16] And their national portable handheld lunch—the Cornish pasty. Even soccer came to Mexico and other parts of the New World along with Cornish miners.[17]

To take on the challenge of emigration, the math must be compelling and the cost of staying far outweighing the costs of leaving. Dropping anchor and coming ashore may be a relief and joy to be celebrated, but also a sorrow to be borne.

I think about how my Cornish ancestors must have mourned, grieving deeply with homesickness and longing for family and friends. But perhaps, upon reaching their new home, they also celebrated by expressing gratitude in worship, kicking a ball, cooking pasties, or otherwise beginning to integrate the life left behind with the new life awaiting. They celebrated to claim who they now were, both sad and happy that their journey was at an end, the anchor dropped.

Anchor Aweigh

The Orton family sails on—return trips to the Caribbean and the Mediterranean. There's scuba diving now. Emily and Erik surf. In 2018, Erik climbed El Capitan, the sheer three-thousand-foot granite tower that overshadows Yosemite National Park. They go to school; they go to work. The Ortons celebrate the rhythm of life and learning.

I like comparing the S Curve to a wave: rising, cresting, crashing, and washing into shore. My conversation with Laird Hamilton, an American big-wave surfer, only reinforces the idea. He says, "Every wave is the beginning. The ride, then the kick out, which is the end, and every wave is its own learning curve because every single wave is different. You immediately separate from yourself. You become a part of the ocean. . . . Nothing quite matches riding a wave."[18]

The ocean holds an unequaled fascination. We can watch its ever-changing face for hours. Every wave is followed by another, and then another. As nineteenth-century French philosopher André Gide wrote, "Each wave owes the beauty of its line only to the withdrawal of the receding one."

It is the same with our growth. Each curve is in part created, and defined, by the one before it and the one that will come after. We've anchored. We may stay in port for a while, but ultimately, we must raise anchor and set sail again.

Anchor Takeaways

This phase typically feels **SLOW**

The next phase of the S Curve of Learning is Anchor. Like a boat coming into harbor, the Anchor stage marks your arrival at the mastery phase. Here, at the high end of your S Curve, you have achieved your objective. Your new behavior is anchored and now a part of you. Your predictive modeling is fluent. Your experience more frequently aligns with your brain's expectations. You feel a sense of completion on this specific S Curve journey. You have arrived.

Here are three things to maximize your growth.

1. Pause and Reflect

When your growth journey is complete, it can be bittersweet. Gratification is mixed with poignance. It may be disorienting, as you wonder where your life will go next. You may realize that the goals that inspired you to reach this point will no longer motivate you going forward. You may miss the old sense of direction, or the old energy. This is the time to pause, to reflect on your journey. Now that the rush of growth is over, you have the unique opportunity to detect patterns that will help you along future S Curves.

Plan your time of pause and reflection to match the significance of this particular curve. Small accomplishments call for a brief anchoring moment at the end of the day. Life milestones (for example, completing an advanced degree, sending kids to college, moving into the C-suite) could precipitate a more extended personal retreat. Think through the phases of your journey and identify the factors that both inhibited and contributed to your growth. Think about the decisions you made and the actions you took. Which ones accelerated your growth? What would you do differently if you could do it again? Take time to reflect on the meaning of this experience, to acknowledge that you have anchored.

2. Celebrate Your Achievement

Once you've paused to consider what you've learned and how you've grown, it is time to celebrate. You did it! Relish this accomplishment. Again, match your celebration to the situation. Celebrate small S Curves by yourself (for example, in a journal or with daily reflection) and/or with people you love. Celebrate the completion of big S Curves with a wider circle of colleagues, family, or friends. Either way, celebrate. Behavioral scientist B. J. Fogg writes, "Celebration is the best way to create a positive feeling that wires in new habits."

3. Prepare for the Next S Curve

With your celebration complete, outline what you'll do next. Is now the time to reconsider compelling opportunities you turned down to stay focused? Are you drawn toward a radically different S Curve such as a career pivot or a move? Anchoring gives you stability and confidence. Chart your next steps from this point of strength. One S Curve flows into another, and then another. Anchor aweigh.

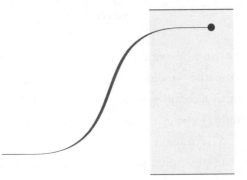

6 Mountaineer

The object of all life is development; and everything that lives has
an inalienable right to all the development it is capable of attaining.

—WALLACE D. WATTLES

Feyzi Fatehi is at the summit of his career and his profession.

He is a computer science pioneer and co-inventor of the world's first commercial real-time database (RTDB) system.[1] A software engineer at Hewlett-Packard in the 1980s, he laid the groundwork for future software applications that can track a space shuttle traveling seventeen thousand miles per hour, or securely execute a stock trade in fifty microseconds. He is the CEO of Corent Technology, a disruptive innovator in cloud migration and modernization, which, compared to old models is "ten times faster, better, and more cost-effective," Fatehi says.[2]

Fatehi's journey to the mastery stage demonstrates, as our previous stories do, that people who are dedicated to making progress, those who want to reach their potential, are not casual trekkers. They're Mountaineers, seeking to summit one learning curve, celebrate their achievement, and then move on to the next S Curve ascent.

As Mountaineers at the top of our S Curve of Learning, we take in the view. We smartly observe where growth was slow, where growth was faster, and how growth on this learning curve is coming to an end. From this vantage point, we can now see the trail we've traversed in its entirety, an illuminating perspective we didn't have before. We spend time surveying and celebrating the accomplishment as Anchors and feel a pang of sadness as a meaningful journey comes to an end.

Where do we go from here?

The answer is simple: find a new mountain to climb. To again experience sweet spot momentum, we need to navigate another launch point. In this chapter we'll discuss the imperative of starting a new S Curve of Learning once we've attained the peak of a curve. We'll see why it's dangerous to set up camp at the top of a learning curve we've mastered. We'll discuss why, in some cases, we may be good at something, but we don't have the heart to keep doing it. Whether we have achieved peak performance on an S Curve or find our ascent abbreviated by the unforeseen, we must descend to ascend again. Understanding every stage of the curve is what allows you to take the summit or regroup when the way is barred. Smart growth requires knowing when you are about to complete a growth cycle and having the courage to embrace a new climb. You are a *Mountaineer*.

View from the Top

Feyzi Fatehi describes himself as having been on a "quest" to learn as much as he could at least since adolescence. Early in his career, he completed an MBA while working at Hewlett-Packard. Over time he worked with several different HP teams, developing peer-to-peer computing, electronic health record systems, each an S Curve to climb. Up he went. Mastery. Celebrate. On to the next climb. "Every two years I . . . kicked myself out of a job," he said. "It was all voluntary, in search of discomfort, and therefore, personal development and growth." But after fourteen years with HP, Fatehi found himself on the top of a curve with nowhere to go: "I felt too comfortable. I always told myself when you feel too comfortable you have to move. . . . It's like in climbing; you can't just camp somewhere. You can rest. You can look around. You can take a deep breath, have a snack. But you've got to keep moving, otherwise you get complacent."

In 1987, Fatehi was invited to climb to the summit of Mt. Whitney in California, the highest mountain in the lower forty-eight US states. This became another launch point for him. The attempt required months of training and preparation. Fatehi's effort distills this lesson, a meaningful metaphor for all S Curve Mountaineers:

> It became a blueprint: if you set a goal, it should be audacious. Bold. It should challenge you to muster all the mental, physical, and emotional training you can. Be prepared for a lot of ups and downs. You reach a peak only to go down the mountain and up another. But with each peak there are new vistas and new beauty you haven't before experienced.

When Fatehi left Hewlett-Packard, he left behind a significant number of stock options and took a 50 percent cut in compensation with a new business, Jamcracker, a pioneer software-as-a-service (SaaS) startup, far ahead of its time. His peers thought he was out of his mind, but Fatehi saw himself in learning decline. He'd felt too comfortable for too long. He needed a new mountain to climb.

The career of British neuroscientist Tara Swart, first introduced in Explorer (chapter 1), illustrates the Mountaineer's challenge.[3] "I grew up in Northwest London," she relates, "the first child of first-generation immigrant Indian parents. I don't remember a time when I didn't think I was going to be a doctor." Swart faced cultural pressure growing up to become a doctor and to live in strict adherence to her family's customs and religious beliefs. She gravitated to psychiatry and neuroscience "in a quest to understand myself—who I really was and what my true purpose would be if I had been free to decide."

Swart earned an MD from Oxford University and a PhD in neuroscience. She and her husband explored the world beyond London: "[W]e moved to Australia, lived in Bermuda, and spent time in South Africa, all of which expanded my worldview and understanding of people and cultures."

Swart excelled as a psychiatrist, but something was missing. She wasn't, in her words, "sweating mentally." Boredom and stagnation were taking root. She said, "I had become increasingly unhappy in my work, worn down by the long hours and the workload, and the sense of not being able to make a real difference to my patients."

It is possible for human beings to stop learning and growing, but it is not possible for them to be content with it. "The entire purpose of the human brain," says neuroscientist Daniel Wolpert, "is to produce movement."[4] You may have experienced this discontent. I know I have. Toward the end of my career as an equity analyst, work was clicking along. I was a well-oiled machine, but my gears weren't engaging as they once had. I hadn't consciously acknowledged it yet, but my Wall Street climb was finished. I was succeeding in the job, but I was failing to continue to grow.

Similarly, Tara Swart left her medical career. She explained, "I looked ahead at the field of psychiatry for the next thirty or forty years and decided that it wasn't going to change." She felt her calling lay elsewhere, toward the spiritual as well as the physiological aspects of the human mind.[5] "When I actually quit my job," Swart recounted, "the chief of psychiatry said to me, 'This is a real loss to us, because you could do this job in your sleep.' And if I needed one last reason to quit," she said, "he had just given it to me."

Many Mountains to Climb

Intrepid Mountaineers will repeatedly undertake challenging S Curve climbs. Tech executive Shellye Archambeau is an inspiring example. In 2013, *Business Insider* named Archambeau the second most influential African American in information technology, citing her stunning reinvention of two struggling companies that ultimately became MetricStream, which makes governance, risk, and compliance (GRC) software.[6] She was the first African American woman to be the CEO of a major Silicon Valley startup.

In the mid-1960s, her family of six moved to a Los Angeles suburb, shortly after the Watts riots. She was the only Black girl in her grade. Children and adults yelled racist slurs at her—a seven-year-old—as she walked to and from school. She suffered a physical attack by two boys in her class. "Nobody driving by stopped," Archambeau says, matter-of-factly.[7]

Despite the obstacles of racism, Archambeau set ambitious and specific goals for her life and career. "I love my clubs," she told her school guidance counselor one day. "American Field Service, National Honor Society, Girl Scouts—you name it—I ultimately will end up leading them." Business, her counselor told her, was much like a club. It was about rallying people around a common goal and getting it done. She responded, "I'm going to go run a business. When I looked at who runs a 'business'— it was chief executive officers—I said, 'I'm going to go be a CEO.' [I] was literally that naive and that audacious."

The CEO peak is a high mountain to climb that comes after scaling multiple mountains en route. After graduating from the Wharton School, Archambeau rose steadily through the sales ranks at IBM. Sales wasn't necessarily her thing, but, "I always looked at the path of the person who was in the job that I wanted. . . . I started out in sales because every CEO at IBM had started in sales," she said.

She rose through the ranks, and ultimately there was an opening for a general manager in IBM's Asia public-sector division. "[I was] the first woman of color to go on an international assignment with IBM," she told me, "which was amazing. This was the '90s, but still I was the first one."

Archambeau knew Asia would be a punishing ascent. She collected feedback:

> My boss [a smart growth leader] who had spent a lot of time working in Asia said to me, "Shellye, how much do you know about being successful in Japan, businesswise?" I said, "I'm reading books, but I'd love your advice." "Three things are critical to success," he said. "The first is wisdom. Wisdom is age." I was in my mid-30s. "The second is being male." I didn't have that either. "And the third one is intelligence. You have only one going for you. You better figure out how to maximize it."

Against the cultural odds, Shellye Archambeau grew this multibillion-dollar division, ranking number one in year-over-year growth. For some, this mountaintop would be accomplishment enough, their climbing days done. But she still had her sights on that higher peak.

The Death Zone

In actual mountaineering, stopping at high altitude can be deadly. Any altitude above 26,000 feet is considered the death zone: an area where bodies and brains start to die from lack of oxygen. Above 26,000 feet, human bodies consume oxygen faster than it can be replenished, a condition known as *anoxia*. Even with supplemental oxygen, physical exhaustion and reduced awareness can lead to serious accidents and death.[8]

Learning is the oxygen of human growth. When learning diminishes, so do we. Learning is essential to our continued development (remember neural plasticity from Accelerator, chapter 3), particularly in adulthood, when the sponge-like mindset we had as children hardens into a more fixed range of assumptions. Unless we engage in new learning opportunities, neural plasticity succumbs to neural rigidity. Precarious as it is, the peak of an S Curve can—ironically—feel like a good place to stop. Getting here was hard. We may be tempted to rest on our learning. But leaving may prove difficult if we linger, and our learning-hungry brain begins to starve.

Journalist Bucky McMahon's brilliantly titled article "Uh-Oh Here Comes the Easy Part" in *Outside* magazine, examines the danger of ease, "When the work seems rote, vigilance slackens, mistakes occur, and sometimes, widows are made. Ask . . . the trekker who, videotaping the final moments of a successful safari, tumbles into a road-construction ditch. They now understand this essential law of adventure travel safety: the dangerous part is past, so prepare yourself."

Boredom is a threat at the top, but so is regression. You might start doing poorly what you learned to do well. The novel information you worked so hard to obtain, chunk by chunk, is already delivered, integrated, and anchored in the vast neural circuitry of the brain. As you moved up the S Curve, you fine-tuned your brain's predictive model, detecting a "just right" degree of novelty: enough to challenge, but not to overwhelm. This met the natural craving for reward via dopamine. That's gratifying at first, but less so as time passes. When the predictive model running in your brain is accurate and what you expect to happen happens, that means no more dopamine rewards for taking a chance and making the right call.[9]

It's true that stagnation can happen at any stage along the curve. Some S Curves just don't offer the opportunity we thought they would. Progress is slow, erratic, or nonexistent. Maybe progress abruptly ends, shy of our objective. But stagnation is most likely to occur at the top of a learning curve. We anchor, we celebrate, we hope the party never ends.

It's understandable. Who doesn't want to be the life of the party, especially when it's *your* party? As you detected patterns in your learning, your receptors became more sensitive to your serotonin levels, which improved your mood. Cortisol levels declined in sync with lower stress. The decision to continue to climb again, to become an Explorer anew, could mean that instead of pleasure, your brain feels pain. Why stop the party to return to that?

Because even celebrating gets tedious after a while, and the party can't last anyway. All the good feelings resulted from the momentum of the sweet spot. Once we reach mastery, it's only a matter of time before we are bored and restless. We need another sweet spot, and that first requires the challenge of a new launch point.

In 1998, Shellye Archambeau knew it was unlikely that she would end up atop Mt. CEO at IBM. So she started looking for a new S Curve mountain to climb. The Blockbuster video franchise—ubiquitous at the time— needed a new president to build Blockbuster.com. Retail operations were moving online in every quarter of the globe. Blockbuster had to keep pace. It needed a leader who could start a dot-com division and launch a website that would ultimately become a movie-streaming platform. "I thought this was the perfect stepping-stone to the CEO job," Archambeau told me. She joined Blockbuster in 1999.

In June of 2000, she quit. Why? Because 2000 was the year Blockbuster CEO John Antico made history as the chief executive who passed on the chance to buy Netflix for 0.001 percent of the company's current value. Netflix, then a fledgling startup, didn't make sense to Antico. Archambeau remembers, "Netflix CEO Reed Hastings and his team came out and essentially pitched, 'Let's take Blockbuster, the brand, and Netflix, the technology, put them together and go conquer the world.' My boss basically laughed at that and said, 'Oh, if that ever becomes something real, we'll just buy them.' . . . It became clear that they really didn't have the vision for where things were heading. That's why I left."

Archambeau descended from her mountain, short of the peak, to regroup at base camp. She caught her breath. By 2002, she was ready to climb again, sights set on the same summit as before: CEO.

It looked like the worst possible time to aspire to anything in the tech world. The dot-com crash had erased some $5 trillion in value from the tech industry. Companies imploded. Archambeau was ready for her CEO job right when the tech sector was littered with newly unemployed CEOs. She realized that if investors thought a company was going to succeed, it would hire a CEO with a track record. So she decided, "I'll go after something that's broken that I can fix," she said.

She became the CEO of Zaplet, a company just months from bankruptcy. She then merged Zaplet with MetricStream, also small and unprofitable, and turned the two around. Since 2008, MetricStream has been a global leader in GRC software. Never stagnant, always the Mountaineer willing to start at the bottom of a new curve, Archambeau achieved the summit of her dreams.

That was fifteen years ago. She's still mountaineering. "I am in what I refer to as my phase two," she told me. She sits on four corporate board directorships (including Verizon and Nordstrom), maintains a growing nonprofit portfolio, and has published a critically acclaimed memoir, *Unapologetically Ambitious*. Her repeat success illustrates that growth leads to more growth. If we are smart about growth, we'll move from one challenging climb to the next.

A fascinating 2019 study titled "The CEO Life Cycle" describes a pattern of growth, stagnation, and possible regrowth over time.[10] Tracking the year-by-year financial performance of more than seven hundred S&P 500 chief executives, the study reveals distinct phases of job performance, beginning with the "honeymoon" period and ending with the "golden years."

Between honeymoons and golden years, however, CEOs will face significant obstacles. Those that survive to year eleven, when the golden years typically begin, must survive the death zone of success first. Attaining the peak of a CEO S Curve, which is, on average, in year six, is "often followed by a time of prolonged stagnation and mediocre results." The plateau becomes a precipice: many CEOs will quit or be fired.

CEOs experience golden years only when they deliberately and repeatedly move to the launch point of new S Curves: "CEOs who survive the complacency trap typically go on to experience some of their best value-creating years."

Freefall: When You Get Pushed Off the Mountain

Even though it's better to get off the mountain under your own power, chances are good that someday you will be on a precipice, and you will get pushed off. It's a rare person who evades this painful experience forever. Some such events will be micro day-to-day upsets, generally reducible to what we intended to accomplish versus what we were in fact able to accomplish. Others will result in a complete paradigm shift, such as when Liz O'Donnell (you met her in Accelerator, chapter 3) chose to recalculate her priorities upon learning that her parents were terminally ill and would require her care for the remaining months of their lives.

But even a shove can have a silver lining. In 1998, Don J. Snyder published a memoir—*The Cliff Walk: A Job Lost and a Life Found*—about his unplanned paradigm shift from a white-collar to a blue-collar career.[11] In 1992, Snyder was an English professor at a prestigious American liberal arts college. He loved his job. His students loved him. He and his wife were expecting their fourth child. They'd just bought a home. The job, university, and community all felt permanent. The Snyders thought they were at Anchor.

Then Snyder was unexpectedly fired. For two long years, he mailed letters to potential employers, in search of a university who needed a talented English professor in midcareer.

Crickets.

Nobody hired him. Snyder descended into depression. He withdrew from his family, from his life. The Snyders sold their "forever" home. The proceeds dwindled, along with their savings. Finally giving up on his academic dream, Snyder took a job as a greenskeeper on a local golf course.

It wasn't half bad. Low stress. Fresh air. Snyder got a construction job next. He knew nothing about the building trade. It wasn't as easy as he'd imagined. Snyder gained a newfound respect for the artistry and complexity of skilled physical labor. He got training, he got paid, he got the satisfaction that comes with exploring and building new competencies. The push that knocked Snyder off Mount Academia allowed him to start growing again. But it took hitting rock bottom for Snyder to climb a new mountain. It also took a conversation with a key influencer in his life: his wife, Colleen McQuinn. Quoting from *The Cliff Walk*:

McQuinn: What do you want to do? You can do whatever you want to.

Snyder: Do you really believe that?

McQuinn: My grandfathers came to this country with barely any education and nothing in their pockets. One made himself into a successful farmer, the other built a happy life as the manager of a grocery store. So, yes.

Snyder: That was a long time ago.

McQuinn: So?

Snyder: Things are harder today.

McQuinn: Do you really think they are? How can they be harder than what they faced? I think you look down on people who just do regular jobs so they can pay their way. I don't. I've never thought one person was better than another person because of the job he does, but I think *you* do. I think you always have.[12]

Snyder now wonders why so many people are dead set on keeping their collars snowy white. Mike Rowe, who you met in the San Francisco sewer, would agree. Many lucrative and rewarding jobs go unfilled while university students rack up astronomical debt, often to discover they finish with no marketable skill.[13] On the S Curve of Learning, there is no hard line between professional and vocational achievement. No matter who you are, where you came from, where you live, or what you do, if you want to progress, the S Curve of Learning applies to you.

Notwithstanding intense preparation before the ascent, mountain climbers can be thwarted by accident, injury, illness, or sudden changes in weather that make it dangerous to proceed. They may not always reach the summit, but they are still Mountaineers.

Similarly, unexpected events can knock us off our S Curve climbs before we reach the pinnacle, even when we still have plenty of learning potential. We've reached *a* summit, but not *the* summit. Layoffs or firings, a business that fails, personal challenges such as divorce, illness, or loss of a key sponsor or loved one can force us to abandon a once-promising climb. Many of these abrupt, involuntary endings, so difficult to navigate at the time, become opportunities for greater growth than we could have imagined. We are still Mountaineers.

Even Feyzi Fatehi was knocked off a curve. In 1982, when he graduated with a BS in engineering from the University of Texas, his dream was a career in the emerging field of solar energy. But emerging fields have their headwinds. Fatehi said, "Right when I graduated, the government eliminated all tax subsidies. Instantly I was disrupted. My dream of becoming a solar engineer—that was the day it died." Without a visa, the sun was about to set on his American dream, too, unless he could find a new launch point. "So, what do you do?" he asked me rhetorically, "as an immigrant, in the pursuit of happiness—and making a living?"

Fatehi had already successfully climbed several substantial S Curves. At age fifteen, he left his home in Iran to study at the Lennox Cook School of English, a private boarding school adjacent to Cambridge University in the UK. The following year, at great sacrifice, his parents made it possible for Fatehi to study in the United States: at the prestigious Hun School in Princeton, New Jersey. Then the BS in engineering.

Then bump. Over the edge of the cliff Fatehi went.

It was the middle of a punishing recession in the United States. Professional level jobs were hard to come by. So, he says, "I did about twenty different jobs. From flipping hamburgers to working at the cash register to catering and project management—whatever I could find."

His precipitous descent also meant going back to school: "I happened to run into a friend of mine who said, 'Hey, next to Austin [Texas] there's a school [Southwest Texas University in San Marcos] that's starting a computer science department and they badly want graduate students.' I said, 'I don't know anything about computer science.' He said, 'That's the point. They're so desperate that they'll accept anyone.'"

When Fatehi finished school for the second (but not final) time, he was hired by HP.

Mountaineers may give up a summit, but you don't give up. You may get booted down the current trail, but you don't stop hitting trails. You are resilient, and that resilience is often accumulated on the path.

By her late twenties, Astrid Tuminez, from the slums of Iloilo City, had summited multiple mountains. One could reasonably expect her to have resilience to spare. Except, because her childhood was focused on day-to-day survival, she grew up feeling that there was no room for failure. "I had this mentality that I can't make mistakes," she says, "If I make mistakes or if I fail, I'm gonna die."

In the late nineties, wanting to learn more about the mysterious workings of money, Tuminez got a job at a Manhattan bank leveraging her fluency in Russian. But then the ruble, among other currencies, collapsed, taking her specialty with it. She said, "I was naively sitting in the Park Avenue office when someone on our tiny trading floor walked up to me, and said, 'You must leave. Now.'"

Anyone who has endured a layoff or firing—and most of us have or will and maybe more than once—will recognize the shock and embarrassment of that moment. (I do.) Tuminez recalls feeling stunned, frightened, and betrayed. She said, "What a disaster. It broke my confidence and my sense of self. . . . It was humiliating. I thought about giving up on trying to learn about money."

Instead, she said, "I'm gonna do this. I'm gonna learn how money works." Tuminez worked her connections in the industry to land a job at insurance giant AIG. "I had a wonderful four years of working on Wall Street doing credit risk and then private equity," she says.

She "failed" but she didn't die. Being fired "helped me become comfortable with failure. It helped me realize I could now let go of this childhood fear." As Tuminez has climbed her various career S Curves, she has climbed an important emotional S Curve—the journey of moving from surviving to thriving.

The Thrill of the Climb

It's not the peak elevation of your S Curve that matters. It's not about whether your mountain is the stuff of legend—an Everest, a Denali. It's about being the guide on your own smart growth journey. You choose the mountain that means the most to you personally. You complete the growth cycle represented by your climb: base camp, climbing route, summit. Only you can know which mountains to climb.

Andreas Goeldi and Bettina Hein are case studies. Their backdrop is the Swiss mountains. Goeldi and Hein are residents of St. Gallen, which lies nestled between Lake Constance and the Alps. You might call Goeldi and Hein a "power couple." Hein is an MIT graduate, law school graduate, and two-time tech company CEO. Goeldi is cofounder and board member of several tech companies headquartered in Switzerland, Germany, and the United States. Goeldi says, "I started in the dot-com boom of the '90s, and experienced the bust in the 2000s." By 2004 his company was back to profitability. As CEO he was receiving considerable acclaim. But he says, "I was deeply unhappy."[14]

"I did a lot of soul-searching," he says. His smart growth epiphany was realizing that his *why* wasn't mountaintops: it was launch points. He said, "I still remember the specific moment. I was walking along the river Limmat that flows through the town of Zurich. I remember the specific spot where I had the insight: I enjoy starting things from scratch. Having a blank sheet of paper."

Andreas Goeldi is a Mountaineer who savors the time in the slow, low-elevation climb rather than the accelerated ascent to the heights. "I missed having nothing," he told me. "Just a couple of cofounders and an empty room." Ecosystems, as we will discuss in the next chapter, are a critical contributor or detriment to growth.

Dislodging Goeldi from his mountaintop involved a combination of intrinsic and extrinsic motivation. Intrinsically, Goeldi was suffering from learning deprivation, craving the thrill of a fresh challenge. Extrinsically, Bettina Hein refused to marry him. She knew he was miserable. She also knew it would be hard to walk away. "There are three things you need to do if you want to get married," she told him. "Number one, get a driver's license. Two, hire a personal assistant. And three, quit your job."

Goeldi accepted her terms. Being a lawyer, Hein (naturally) wanted it in writing. "I actually drew it up on paper as a contract, because I had just finished my law degree and needed to use my skills. But it wasn't just for me," she added. "I could see how hellish it was for him."

Goeldi and Hein got married. He launched a new company, this time as chief technical officer. He said, "After spending several years as a CEO of a company with several hundred people, I went back to writing code every day."

People were "quite surprised," by his unconventional choice, he told me. But those closest to him knew that a from-scratch technical role was a better fit for Goeldi's sense of purpose. Good Mountaineers don't have to take on all the tallest peaks. Like Goeldi, we can gain a clearer perspective of what sort of Mountaineer we are by returning to our *why*. Hein summarizes, "What I've learned over my entrepreneurial career is that you constantly have to disrupt yourself."[15]

Smart growth means getting off the mountaintop before the universe gives you the nudge, if you can control that timing. It requires having a growth mindset, and being open to possibilities outside your norm, like a graphic designer taking his young family to sea or a girl from the slums deciding she wants to learn Russian.

Descend to Ascend Again

If you hike even occasionally, you know that coming down exercises different muscles than going up does. This is also true of S Curves of Learning, whether you're coming down from the top, or have chosen or been forced to descend from an earlier stage in your journey. Mountaineers know it's different to get down than it is to go up, and difficult in its own way.

Feyzi Fatehi felt the sting of sacrificing financial advantages at Hewlett-Packard when he descended to explore new S Curves in startups. Shellye

Archambeau felt the frustration of not quite reaching the peak at Blockbuster to find another mountain that promised her a better shot at the summit. Once Andreas Goeldi realized he loved the launch, he felt the liberation of getting off a curve he no longer loved to start from scratch as a CTO. Tara Swart walked away from being a physician to heal herself. Astrid Tuminez was humble enough to ask for help.

In one of the closing scenes of his famous *Lord of the Rings* fantasy trilogy, author J. R. R. Tolkien depicted the departing sage, Gandalf, offering his final wisdom to the hero-king Aragorn. Gandalf is leaving the mortal world forever. He has led Aragorn partway up a rugged mountain. Behind them stretches the vista of Aragorn's kingdom of Gondor, newly liberated from chaos and war. Aragorn wishes Gandalf would stay. What will become of his successors, Aragorn wonders, without Gandalf there to guide them?

"Turn your face from the green world," says Gandalf, "and look where all seems barren and cold."

Aragorn looks. There on the barren slope grows a white sapling, long thought to be extinct. This image always reminds me that the best things that grow can be discovered, not on the air-starved mountaintop, but on the arduous, joyful climb.

Mountaineer Takeaways

This phase typically feels **SLOW**

The sixth stage in your S Curve of Learning is Mountaineer: one who embraces the adventure of the climb. As a Mountaineer you are dedicated to learning and personal growth. You are not a casual trekker. You don't limit yourself to Sunday strolls, or even the occasional hike. You tackle mountains. This stage is about climbing many micro S Curves as part of a life devoted to S Curve climbing.

View from the top: This stage in your smart growth is marked by a sense of satisfaction at reaching the top and curiosity about what's next. As a

Mountaineer, you seek to summit one learning curve, celebrate your achievement, then plan the next S Curve ascent. From the top, you can look back and see where growth was slow, where growth was faster and, now that you've incorporated this S Curve into your identity, how growth may stall. Mountaineering is marked by two elements.

The Peril of Stagnation

At this stage of success, two dangers lurk:

1. **Freefall.** The unexpected push or slip may come when complacency soothes you into letting down your guard or when other unexpected life events arise. Reaching the mountain top, the top of the S Curve, is perilous precisely because that's when you tend to stop paying attention. When you slip or are pushed off by the unexpected, remember that you've reached *a* summit, but not *the* summit.

2. **The death zone.** In physical mountaineering, staying at a high altitude can be deadly because there isn't enough oxygen to sustain life. Stagnation can happen at any stage, but you are at the greatest risk during this final stage of your growth because you've exhausted the potential for growth in this specific S Curve. The dopamine rewards associated with refining your brain's predictive model have helped fuel your climb to this point. But now that you are getting what you expect, you experience few to no brain chemistry rewards, and you risk boredom. Things again feel slow.

Learning is the oxygen of human growth. When learning diminishes, so do we.

The Thrill of the Climb

Smart growth is filled with many S Curves, many climbs. Plan your next mountain to climb before you stagnate, fall, or get pushed off the summit of your current S Curve. Keep three things in mind as you consider your next steps:

1. Not all summits are reached. Sometimes your climb is interrupted by factors outside your control from either work (for example, getting

laid off, fired, a business failure) or your personal life (for example, divorce, illness, or loss of a loved one or key supporter). These hardships can force you to abandon a once-promising S Curve. Even though this is a part of life largely outside your control, it can still feel like failure. This death of your dreams is extremely painful, but with resilience, you will climb again.

2. Descend to ascend again. A growth mindset means being willing to descend from a mountaintop achievement and become a beginner again on a new S Curve. Just as hiking downhill uses different muscles than hiking uphill, learning to successfully descend from the summit allows you to tackle a new S Curve and continue your smart growth.

3. Create, don't compete. If you're focusing on creating rather than competing, you will always win. The best of life is not found in the rare moments of mountaintop accomplishment, but in the everyday effort of joyful learning and growth.

As a meaningful journey comes to a poignant end, where do you go from here? The answer is simple: you climb a new mountain. To experience sweet spot momentum again, you need to navigate another launch point.

Mastery Summary for Smart Growth Leaders

For individuals in mastery, predictive models are accurate, behavior is anchored, and confidence is high. Support and good judgment are plentiful. With things comfortable and familiar, stress levels are relatively low. But because this growth curve has become a part of who they are, growth is and feels *slow*.

For a summary of what mastery feels like, see the following Goldilocks Table. The chair is no longer just right, it has become too small. A new chair, possibly a new table, is in order. When you as a leader understand the experience people are having atop the S Curve, you can help create conditions where they can be successful in this phase of their growth.

GOLDILOCKS TABLE

Plotting the Emotional Journey of Growth

Dimensions	Launch Point: Slow	Sweet Spot: Fast	Mastery: Slow
Confidence	The feeling of confidence is seldom aligned to reality at the launch. Some personalities will feel no confidence in this new area and fight imposter syndrome and insecurities that drain their energy. Other personalities will feel more confident than their limited experience warrants, leading to costly and avoidable mistakes.	As you gain experience, the overconfidence or imposter syndrome (depending on personality) tends to fade and confidence strengthens.	Your confidence has been strengthened by time and multiple tests.
Identity	Difficult and deep questions emerge: • I'm not good at this. Do I have value? • Is doing something like this aligned with who I am . . . or even want to be?	The difficult questions have faded: "I'm good at this!" . . . but it's not an established part of your identity yet.	The old questions are gone; you've been so good at this for so long that it's part of who you are. New questions emerge: • Do I want more? • Is there more? • What else could I do?
Familiarity	Much about this area is brand new, like exploring a new country. Past experience in other areas can provide valuable orientation but should be treated cautiously so you don't miss the important details and differences.	This area is mostly familiar but still has some newness and novelty.	This area is very familiar and comfortable—home-field advantage.

Dimensions	Launch Point: Slow	Sweet Spot: Fast	Mastery: Slow
Mental state	Some personalities find this stressful, feeling overwhelmed by the volume of new information to process and things to learn. Other personalities find all the new stimuli exhilarating. Both sides need to keep these tendencies from pulling them off the path of deliberate growth.	You have just the right balance of familiar information or tasks and new challenges. In many cases, the experience is one of flow state where you are fully immersed and have an enjoyable feeling of energized focus and full involvement.	Boredom is a key risk at this stage because there aren't enough new challenges (e.g., new things to learn, new information to process) to sustain engagement and motivation.
Value proposition	Considerable untapped potential waits on the other side of the investment. Uncertainties remain, but the reward seems worth it.	You are actively realizing much of the potential, and additional opportunities remain. Uncertainty is considerably lessened because of the momentum you've built in this stage.	Most of the potential to be gained through direct involvement has been realized. New opportunities for rewards related to teaching or mentoring emerge.
Successful mindset	Success at this stage flows from leaning into the challenge: saying yes and experimenting with new approaches, ways of being, and relationships.	You shift from always saying yes and broad experimentation to learning to say no so that you can focus and execute.	You say yes to new challenges or opportunities to find new rewards and escape boredom and entitlement. You mentor others, find new dimensions of excellence, try something else entirely.
Support network	A supportive network might be available, but you generally don't know who is in the network or how to access them . . . even if you did, you're not sure you'd want to because you don't want to look needy.	You know who to ask for help, when to ask, and how to best leverage help and are comfortable asking for help.	Your support network is stronger than ever with the added dimension that now you're often providing help to others.

(continued)

Dimensions	Launch Point: Slow	Sweet Spot: Fast	Mastery: Slow
Decision approach	The tendency for most is to directly follow the procedure and guidance of authority figures.	You are able to recognize levels of uncertainty in authority figures and different situations and contexts.	You are able to anticipate and reflect on the situation given your experience and make a wise judgment that is tailored to specific needs and context.
Knowledge base	You are starting to learn important facts and the needed language . . . but not enough to be efficient or effective. You can think you know more than you do because you don't know what you don't know.	You know how to be efficient and effective. You increasingly know what you don't know.	You know not just how to be efficient and effective, but also the principles and theory behind the methods. You know so much by intuition that much of what you know is largely unconscious.
Energy and output	For most, this new challenge takes more energy than you expected, and the progress is slower than expected.	You can get more done with less energy than ever; the momentum is exhilarating and there is no end in sight.	You can still get more done with less energy when you apply yourself, but it's not generally as exhilarating as it was in the sweet spot.

Grow Your People: Managing People at Mastery

Individuals in mastery are competent and productive. They have a sense that their work matters, have overcome obstacles, and experienced advocacy and support to reach this summit.

They are the pillars of a team, frequently sought out for advice.

The old questions around identity are gone. But new ones may emerge. *I'm good at what I do, but why do I feel like I can't keep doing this? Is there more for me?* Boredom is a key risk. In our data set, a significant percentage of the people in mastery in their current role reported being very bored.

What your people now need from you is a challenge, ideally inside of your organization. Even better, if you can help them turn what looks like a summit on their current S Curve into the base camp of a new one. Whether it's new projects and team configurations that expand their skill set or tapping into a larger purpose, it must be a grander *why* that allows them to expand their influence and reach across your organization.

Below is a summary table of how to manage people in mastery based on both the career stage of the individual and the type of organization in which you work.

HOW TO MANAGE PEOPLE AT MASTERY

Leading at Mastery Theme: CHALLENGE

	TYPE OF ORGANIZATION		
	Young and/or growing	**Advancing and/or midstage**	**Historic and/or complex**
Early career	When you create an environment where early in their career, individuals believe this is *a* summit, not *the* summit, you will build a strong pipeline. "There is always another mountain to climb" is critical to keeping these team members motivated. Think about lateral and divergent moves to facilitate growth. There will be blockages in growing your pipeline. Keep the conversation open. Emphasize that iteration and experimentation are frequently necessary to find the right fit.	The career paths for rising talent are ever expanding. Investing in this group means they know you care, you have their back, and you want the best for them. Be careful not to overemphasize promotions. The best next mountain may actually be approaching this current role with a fresh approach or a lateral move. Even if change cannot be constant, communication can be consistent.	There can be a false sense of mobility within large organizations; early-career masters frequently hit points of frustration when new curves don't come as quickly as they would like. Develop a culture where people believe they can figure it out and find a way with their career. This engineering of a career may involve stepping back to grow. This develops resilience, strengthening the core of the organization. New curves sometimes take the form of professional development and more connection points across the organization.

(continued)

	TYPE OF ORGANIZATION		
	Young and/or growing	**Advancing and/or midstage**	**Historic and/or complex**
Midcareer	In young and/or small organizations, everyone is responsible for doing everything. Your midcareer team members can be organizational linchpins, given their tremendous and still-growing capacity. They want to make a meaningful contribution. Give them a mountain to climb—a significant challenge.	Don't take midcareer high performers for granted. You rely on their technical expertise and leadership skills: they rely on you to appreciate and to challenge them. Create thoughtful touchpoints for both individuals and teams to ensure that their mastery is being leveraged, valued, and celebrated.	Established companies tend to have structures in place for early-career masters, whether divergent paths and/or leadership development. But midcareer experts are often left to self-advocate—to find and climb the mountain themselves. Work to develop a culture for midcareer professionals where lateral moves are celebrated and also seen as momentum builders—as "onward and upward."
Expert career	Experts in new or small organizations are critical. You brought in someone at the top of their curve because you needed their expertise. You are climbing a new mountain and need an expert guide. Whether they leave you at this summit or continue with you to the next mountain, ensure that they help you build in-house capability.	Experts who are also in the mastery phase in a role are frequently viewed as the establishment. These individuals wield influence and embody your company's culture. Understand what motivates them. This will help you know when these masters need a new challenge, to begin a new growth cycle. As your organization grows, access to you can be difficult. Create access points so you are hearing and receiving their input. Individuals in the mastery phase need affirmation too.	Leaders sometimes fail to have conversations about career paths with experts. They are afraid that if they ask the expert in the mastery phase what they want, "they will tell me they need or want something I can't give." Perhaps leaders want a promotion, but often they simply want affirmation, and an update or recalibration of their current role so they can continue to make progress. Matching what the organization needs to the role this expert wants to play is what makes them valuable. Don't lose talent because you didn't have the conversation.

Additional Tips for Managers

- **Celebrate milestones.** The tendency in most companies is to stay focused on production and forget to stop and acknowledge accomplishments. Recognizing movement is important. We were made for movement, but when we pause, as happens every night when we sleep, we consolidate our gains and reinforce what we've learned. Celebration is about *seeing* people, as we do when we celebrate a birthday. It marks the end of one S Curve while giving permission to begin a new one. Remember, emotions create habits.

- **Examine expectations.** Where people perceive they are in their growth is an internal experience. You may not think they are in the mastery phase, but they think they are. Understand why. When they take the S Curve assessment and show up in mastery, it warrants a conversation.[1] They may be in this place because of domain expertise but still feel challenged. If they don't feel challenged, they are at risk of flight or complacency. Based on our data, approximately one-third of individuals in the mastery phase are bored. For retention and succession purposes, where workers perceive they are in their own growth is more important than how their managers see it.

  Sidenote: One thing to consider. Sometimes people are unhappy, not because they haven't moved to a new S Curve, but because others were allowed to. Look for your own blind spots. Are you an equal opportunity manager?

- **Set your ego aside.** Some employees will actively seek new opportunities. As a manager, it takes a tremendous amount of ego for this not to feel personal. It's part of why it is so hard for people to move internally. Egos get in the way. But any internal move will require brokering and facilitation. Is it possible for people to move in your organization? Is it possible for people to move from your team? Do you allow for and advocate growth? If not, what expectations of your own need to be managed? If people think you are trying to fob off weak players onto their team, give them a money-back guarantee. You are sponsoring this move because it's right for the organization and for them, even though it will be a setback for you. If they don't want the people after three months, you will happily take them back.

- **Encourage an external expedition.** Sometimes it's your job to push people to new S Curves. Maybe they are ready to move on and they don't know it yet. Maybe their S Curve no longer fits with what your organization needs. Be clear and kind—just as you would want others to be with you. This honors their dignity. Once the decision is made, ask what they want to do—and how you can support them. We learned during the pandemic that we are more resilient than we thought. Make your decision. Then let them decide.[2]

Grow Your Company: Mastery Implications for Leaders

Below we provide specific ways to apply the S Curve of Learning model and the S Curve Insight Platform to grow your organization.[3]

- To orient your team for growth, a minority (i.e., less than 20 percent) of your team should be in the mastery stage. Team members in this stage are frequently domain experts who can perform at high levels and also have the deep well of experience needed to inform difficult judgment calls and provide valuable mentoring.

- Use the S Curve Insight Platform to track where people perceive they are in their growth—and to inform how you can support them in their growth. The tool helps spark an engaging and deliberate conversation. Is an individual showing up in the mastery phase, but fully engaged because they are finding new dimensions of excellence? Or are they feeling a need to stretch beyond this current role, excellence notwithstanding? In conversation, decide how best to grow this individual to grow your company.

- Take stock of what resources are available to challenge individuals in mastery. While too many people in the mastery phase can create a crowded mountaintop, tipping the scale toward stagnation, high-growth companies will have a healthy distribution of people and teams who have the expertise to match the mountain you are climbing.

- Climbing together. People in the mastery stage have a more expansive perspective and typically have relationships across an organization. They are in a position to drive collaboration. We often talk about evolution as being a competitive activity, survival of the fittest, but without collaboration and cooperation, no progress would be made.

- Up and down the mountain. Experienced Mountaineers can do S Curve loops—heading back down the mountain to help those in the sweet spot and launch point along. These S Curve loops can not only create conditions that lead to innovation, but because of the tremendous exertion required, they can be the challenge that keeps your masters engaged. This can be meaningful for the person in Mastery and productive for others.

- If your team does get "out of balance" and heavily weighted toward mastery, small shifts (new projects, coaching/mentoring responsibilities, tackling BIG problems that you might typically manage on your own) can create opportunities for a team to reset and pull mastery people back into the sweet spot.

Growing an organization is like baking bread. Bread needs enough yeast, water, and sugar in order to rise. If it doesn't rise long enough, you get what the pioneers called hardtack. If you let it rise too long, it collapses. The rising of the bread is called proving. We are proving ourselves. Part of the magic (and challenge for engaged managers to learn) is that the bread does much of the work on its own. Start with raw ingredients, hiring for potential. As people grow, challenge them, appreciate them. Once they have risen, before they collapse, give them something new to do. Whether you lead a team of ten or ten thousand, you are in a position to help people rise.

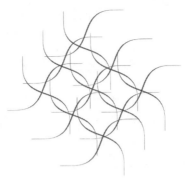

7 Ecosystem

In nature nothing exists alone.

—RACHEL CARSON

Now that we have traversed the S Curve, conducting a forensic analysis of each successive stage of growth, it's time to talk holistically. The earlier chapters have prefigured this final one, where we will examine the importance of our growth ecosystem.

Ponds of water lilies are unique ecosystems composed of many elements: water, soil, sunlight, nutrients, other flora, and fauna too: frogs, turtles, snakes, fish, birds. These all interact in complex ways: fish and turtles find shade and cooler water under the lily pads while also nibbling at the plants, pruning them, lengthening the time the lilies can flourish without overrunning the available space. Turtles and frogs can sun themselves atop the lily pads, the frogs enjoying a tasty meal of roving bugs. Perhaps the pond could do without snakes (my preference), but the snakes cannot do without the pond.

We aren't, of course, lilies in a pond. But just as the lily is inseparable from the pond, we—all of us—live, work, and grow in relation to other elements. We constantly draw resources from and contribute to our S Curve ecosystems.

The Human Element

We take for granted how the physical elements of our environment affect us. Sunlight is an easy example. It is key to producing serotonin, which fights off depression, and melatonin, which affects our circadian sleep-wake cycle. Something as simple as a window will elevate your work space, your mood, your livelihood. The paint color on your wall can also improve your mood, influencing your productivity. A window is a good investment; a change of paint is good therapy.

But people aren't like paint. We can't simply change out a person to improve our mood. Our interconnectedness with others—the relatedness that we talked about in Accelerator, chapter 3—is what makes our ecosystem work.

Florence Knoll Bassett is a case study. For two decades, Florence was the driving creative force behind Knoll Associates, a New York City design firm that produces office systems, files and storage, seating, tables, and desks.

Born Florence Schust in 1917, an only child, her father was an immigrant engineer and baker who died when she was five.[1] Her mother died when Florence was twelve. But her mother had the foresight to designate family friend Emil Tessin as Florence's legal guardian.[2] Tessin took Florence on a driving tour of the Upper Midwest of the United States to explore boarding schools she could attend. At the Kingswood School for Girls in Bloomfield Hills, Michigan, Florence saw "home." The beauty of the building and the design of its interior spaces spoke to her, and it was populated with like-minded young ladies interested in the arts and gifted instructors. It was a promising place for Florence to pursue her education and develop her talents.

Emil Tessin was a foundational element in Florence's early ecosystem. Tessin encouraged young Florence to investigate schools for herself, and he gave her the autonomy to make her own choice. Choosing Kingswood School wasn't blind luck. It was the result of launch point exploration resulting in an astute choice.

Kingswood was a recent addition to the Cranbrook Academy of Art, one of the top art, architecture, and design institutions in the United

States. It was led by, and designed by, Eliel Saarinen, a giant in the Arts and Crafts movement and an influential twentieth-century architect.

Florence's profound interest in architecture and design began to unfurl in Kingswood's beautiful spaces. Saarinen took notice. He and his wife, Loja, became informal parents to the orphaned girl. Their children, Pipsan and Eero (the latter became a famed architect himself), befriended her. They took her on summer holidays. They spent leisure time at the family home in Helsinki; she was immersed in the art, architecture, and culture of Europe. Eliel and Eero Saarinen became permanent fixtures in Florence's personal and professional ecosystems, and she did in theirs. With the Saarinens' patronage, Florence secured opportunities to study with several of the great architects of the day: Walter Gropius, Marcel Breuer, Ludwig Mies van der Rohe.[3]

Nineteenth-century American sculptor Harriet Hosmer said, "The great thing in every profession . . . is to get a good 'start,' then all is right. I never read the life of any artist who did not date the rising of their lucky star from the hand of some beneficent friend or patron."[4] The Saarinens were critical contributors to Florence's early ecosystem. In 1941, at twenty-four, Florence Schust took her stellar credentials and ecosystem relationships to New York City, bent on becoming an architect.

Virtuous (Not Vicious) Growth Cycles

More on Florence soon, but first notice how all the stories in this book play out against the backdrop of an ecosystem. Some people, like Florence Knoll Bassett, despite being an early orphan, are lucky to land in a pond rich with resources, with plenty of carrying capacity. For others, like Astrid Tuminez from Iloilo City, resources are limited. Their rhizome may be anchored in the mud of an impoverished puddle of a slum. Even with abundant ability and determination, Astrid Tuminez couldn't grow on her own. No one can. It's not just artists who need beneficent friends and patrons. Tuminez needed her overburdened teenage sister and nuns, among others. "No person in this world is self-made," she said to me. "It's a delusion."

That's why we are talking about ecosystems as our final chapter. We'll start with what we need from our ecosystem to grow, depending on where we are on our current S Curve (we have talked about how to grow our people at the end of each major section). We'll then consider the ecosystems that made the S Curve stories in this book possible. We will discuss not what we are getting from our ecosystem, but rather what we are giving to it.

In talking about how we learn, leap, and repeat, there has been an implicit assumption that these are virtuous growth cycles. In our case studies, the interactions of various elements in the ecosystem lead to growth for all participants in the ecosystem. But not all ponds are like that. A stagnant pond can become covered with surface scum and algae, sometimes toxic algae that can kill animals (and humans) who drink the water. The algae become food for bacteria that use up the available oxygen, causing the fish and aquatic insects to die. A vicious cycle of decay sets in. Cancer is another example of a vicious growth cycle, where malfunctioning malignant cells proliferate, preventing benign cells from normal growth, while also excreting toxic chemicals that damage or kill body tissues. Human ecosystems can have toxic elements as well, usually in the form of people who poison the work or living environment with their bad conduct, pursuing their own growth at the expense of others.

By talking about and acknowledging those who make it possible for us to grow, and the importance of helping others grow, I'm making it explicit that this book is about virtuous, not vicious, growth cycles. Not dumb, but smart growth.

In New York, the adult Florence had options. But not as many as we might think, at least not initially. Despite her education, experience, and powerful network, the larger ecosystem wasn't particularly hospitable to women's achievement. In 1941 America, women weren't architects. They weren't designers. At best they were decorators, and rarely professional ones. "I am not a decorator," became Florence's refrain. I suspect that the economic and employment conditions created by World War II helped her get her foot in the door at a design firm. Women seeking a professional opportunity suddenly found openings—temporarily. After the war, she'd have likely struggled to stay on at a firm if she hadn't fortuitously met Hans Knoll.

Hans Knoll wandered into Florence's firm, looking for customers. He was a recent immigrant to the United States, and founder of Hans G. Knoll Furniture Company. Florence had the autonomy to choose who she worked for, and soon she was working for Hans. They became collaborators, then business partners. They reinvented themselves, combining Hans's furniture with Florence's cutting-edge interior design, and rebranded the business as Knoll Associates. In 1946, they married.

Though details of their story are scarce, it's clear Hans recognized and promoted Florence's gifts. He seemed to understand the value of the ecosystem in a real way. His somewhat unusual decision (at the time) to let his wife have an equal seat at the table, sometimes taking a back seat to her, was the critical part of the ecosystem that made Florence's superlative artistic contributions possible. Wise decisions about whom we work for, work with, and partner with in our professional and personal lives help us create an ecosystem where all participants can grow.

Writing in *Lean In*, Facebook COO Sheryl Sandberg says, "I truly believe that the single most important career decision that a woman makes is whether she will have a life partner and who that partner is."[5] A good choice of life partner doesn't matter just for women. Warren Buffett makes the case as well, for all of us: "You want to associate with people who are the kind of person you'd like to be. You'll move in that direction. And the most important person by far in that respect is your spouse. I can't overemphasize how important that is."[6]

Florence and Hans were a dynamic partnership. One of Florence's lasting innovations was the Knoll Planning Unit. KPU's holistic design approach has become standard in the industry, where teams work to harmonize all aspects of a building's design rather than making ad hoc changes. Spatial organization, furniture style and arrangement, lighting, fabrics, and colors are all integrated according to the designer's overarching scheme. KPU came close to fulfilling Florence's vision of human-friendly "total design."[7]

Tragically, Hans Knoll died in a car accident in 1955, just nine years after they married. He was forty-one. Eero Saarinen eulogized him, first commending Hans's contribution to the world of interior design, then adding,

"[Hans] dealt with each employee in a personal, human way. To designers he gave generously of his own creative imagination, encouraging them to undertake new and better things. He always freely gave credit to his designers, yet he—who played a big part in their work—never took any credit himself. The generosity, the enthusiasm, the inspiration and the concern for human beings . . . will long be remembered."[8] Hans Knoll cultivated an environment where his employees could grow. As they grew, so did the business.

After Hans's death, Florence took the helm as president until she sold the company in 1960. In 1961, she became the first woman to receive the Gold Medal for Industrial Design from the American Institute of Architects. Knoll Associates was a leading design house globally, speeding along in the sweet spot. But perhaps Florence was at the top of her S Curve. After marrying Harry Hood Bassett, she relocated to Miami, becoming part of a new ecosystem, and cutting daily ties with the design community of Knoll Associates (some of whom, including her beloved friend Eero Saarinen, had passed away). She sought freedom to focus entirely upon her métier, architecture and design. Today, her work for Knoll is displayed in museums and treasured in private collections. After leaving Knoll, for the rest of her long and productive life—she passed away in 2019, at the age of 101—Florence would quietly work on projects for personal clients only.

Who and What We Need Changes

At the launch point of an S Curve, we can't depend on serendipitous events or the right people magically appearing. We may get lucky, but it's just as likely we will have to fashion our own luck through strategy. When we can choose the elements in our ecosystem, particularly the human ones, we should. Purposefully ask, "Who and what will help me grow?" and "Who can I invest in? How can I help others grow?"

Researchers Karen Fingerman and Melinda Blau compare our networks of people to a convoy on the move, "A handful of people travel alongside you for miles. The peripheral people, neither family nor close friends, your consequential strangers, are often there for a particular segment of the trip and tend to serve specific needs." Our ability to bring people into the convoy is critical to our S Curve journey. Likewise, learning to be a meaningful fellow traveler in the convoys of others is an intrinsic factor in smart growth. "Our convoys," they conclude, "represent our history and our potential."[9]

Change is inevitable and necessary in an ecosystem. Those contributing to our growth as an Explorer may lose their utility or become unavailable as we become an Accelerator. People important to us at the Collector stage may not be present at the Metamorph stage. We need different types of relationships at different stages on our curve. On the launch point, we need support: teachers, trainers, and truth tellers to help us explore and collect data to determine whether we should continue on a particular curve. People like Florence's mother, or Emil Tessin, and benefactors like the Saarinens, who were the foundation of Florence's early life. We need guides to urge us on, to keep our spirits up when progress is slow, to pick us up if we fall down, or if a curve becomes unworkable.

In the sweet spot, we need focus. We need people to honor our growing need for autonomy, coaching us as we gain in competence and stature—Hans Knoll. The best advisers will also raise the red flag when necessary, not because they're obstructive, but because they care enough when our need for speed (and a possible lack of focus) could lead to a crash.

In the mastery phase, we need people who can celebrate with us as we drop anchor on our new self (a role Harry Hood Bassett, Florence's second husband, hopefully played in her ecosystem as she won awards that Hans didn't live to see). We also need people who will give us a nudge to move on, to demand more of ourselves—people who help us pick the next mountain and start the climb.

The Person behind Your S Curve

In my podcast interviews, I've noticed again and again how guests credit teachers with creating ecosystems where people thrive and can pursue smart growth lives.

Remember Mike Rowe, the originator of *Dirty Jobs* from Explorer, chapter 1? Rowe would never have ventured into the sewer, would never have stood in front of a camera, if it were not for a teacher. He said, "I had a music teacher in high school named Mr. King, who took me metaphorically by the scruff of the neck and changed the trajectory of my thinking." King was an ex-boxer. "A force of nature," in Rowe's words. But hiding under his prickly exterior was a smart growth leader who cared about giving young Explorers the guidance they needed to launch and to thrive.

One of the things that surprised me most was learning that Rowe—future host of thousands of hours of TV programming—had a stutter. Rowe said, "When [King] realized that, he assigned me a solo in a song because you don't stutter when you sing."[10]

Then Fred King pushed him to audition for a school play. "This was impossible," Rowe observed, "I had a stammer, I was kind of shy. I had no interest in being on stage. But he demanded it, and I trusted him. This is one of those moments that I look back on and think, 'Oh, that was important.' He reoriented me. He got me to ask, 'What if I were a seventeen-year-old kid who isn't afraid to sing?'"

Without Fred King, there might be no *Dirty Jobs*—no Mike Rowe, the charismatic Explorer extraordinaire of reality TV. Rowe changed the entertainment ecosystem because King changed the ecosystem of a small high school in Anywhere, USA. King's tough-love encouragement brought Rowe out of his shell. He changed Rowe's life. And in some ways, Rowe has changed the world.

Teachers, parents, coaches, colleagues, partners, and managers can all be (or not) smart growth leaders.

What if, for example, Mikaila Ulmer's parents had said, "just stay away from bees," after she was stung twice in a week? A perfectly normal response! But Ulmer's parents were focused. They took the time to teach their daughter about the ecosystem of insects; a multimillion-dollar company followed.

What if Maria Merian's stepfather had said, "Caterpillars are disgusting. Stick to the cleaning. Women don't paint."

What if Zaza Pachulia's first NBA coaches—Doc Rivers with the Orlando Magic, Jason Kidd with the Milwaukee Bucks—had benched a rookie immigrant with a substandard vertical jump? Instead, like smart growth

leaders in any industry, they spotted his potential, trained, and encouraged him. Zaza was an integral part of a Golden State Warriors team that won two NBA championships.

Jason Licht didn't tell Michelle McKenna that it was impossible to conduct the entire 2020 NFL draft online. He said it would be hard. He said the time frame was brutal. But he trusted McKenna, the NFL's CIO, and she trusted him. They leveraged their resources through the type of human-to-human connection that precipitates breakthroughs. They created a subsystem never seen before: the virtual draft.

Emily Orton didn't say "get a real job" when her husband, Erik, recently laid off, proposed they pack up the kids and go to sea. Erik wasn't born a sailor. He was a graphic designer with a queasy stomach. This wasn't Emily's dream (initially), but Emily was present, so present that when the family literally found themselves in the same boat, Emily navigated a ten-month trek from the Caribbean to New York City, a challenge even for experienced sailors.

Shellye Archambeau's boss at IBM didn't say, "Traditional Asian culture is patriarchal. You're too young and inexperienced. You haven't got a prayer working in Japan." Instead, he pointed out the quality that could help Archambeau conquer the challenge: her intelligence. The future general manager of IBM Asia's public-sector services—the future CEO of MetricStream—started her climb with a solid, yet caring push.

What if Hans Knoll hadn't been willing to cede the spotlight at a time when women rarely played leading roles in companies? By recognizing his wife's potential, Knoll collaborated with her to create a groundbreaking design firm in which Florence's genius could flourish.

Remember Harry Kraemer, whom we met at the beginning of this book? Kraemer gave many an employee the solid-yet-caring push when he was CEO at Baxter International. But first, Kraemer got the push himself, from his own ecosystem-minded CEO.

Back when he was first working for Baxter—a young analyst with just a few months on the job—Kraemer's manager charged him with valuing Baxter's proposed acquisition of another company. How much was the target company worth? How much should they offer?[11]

The target company was worth $50 million, Kraemer reckoned. He drafted his report. "I turned it in to my boss [Jerry] who said, 'Harry, that's fantastic. You did a great job.'"

Feeling gratified (and curious), Kraemer asked Jerry if he knew how much Baxter was going to offer for the company. "Jerry said, 'We're gonna pay $100 million. . . .' Now I was a little confused." Jerry had just told Harry he'd done a good job. So, who was making the $100 million call?

Jerry's answer: "Those guys."

"Who are 'those guys'?" Kraemer was persistent. His boss recited the org chart. The division president must have made the call. And if not, then the CFO. And if not the CFO, then the CEO, Vernon R. Loucks, must have made it.

"What if I happen to run into him?" Kraemer ventured.

"Harry, it's done," Jerry replied.

The odds of junior analyst Harry Kraemer running into Loucks were slim, right? Kraemer shares, "What [Jerry] didn't realize . . . is that when the CEO was in town . . . at 7:00 every morning he'd go into the cafeteria to grab a grapefruit. So, the next morning, quarter to seven, I'm sort of hanging around the grapefruit."

Loucks showed up. Kraemer pounced. You can probably guess what he wanted to talk about. Kraemer introduced himself. He steered the small talk toward the valuation. Loucks wanted to know what his obscure analyst thought about the offer.

"I said, 'It's a nice company, but I'm having a hard time coming up with it being worth more than $50 million.'"

Loucks was intrigued. Whom did Harry work for, he wanted to know. Harry worked for Jerry. "Grab Jerry," Loucks ordered. "Come on up to my office at 11 o'clock. We can talk about it."

Harry, Jerry, and Vernon talked about it. Baxter revised its offer. Kraemer felt gratified again, to have his intelligence taken seriously by a seriously intelligent CEO. Then Loucks gave Harry a push: "Make sure you challenge [the boss]. Whatever role you're in. You've got to ask questions. Challenge them."

It was a teaching moment Kraemer never forgot. Don't reflexively accept the decision of your so-called superior. Trust your own judgment and

assert it. Loucks meant to foster an ecosystem where smart employees didn't get shut down. He wanted an ecosystem where valuable information didn't get overlooked, whatever the employee's role might be. Because Kraemer questioned his leaders, a company saved $50 million, and a future CEO was nudged up the curve.

Stocking the Pond

How do we ensure we are part of a virtuous growth cycle, not a vicious one? Consider Redfish Lake, high in the Sawtooth Mountain range in Idaho. This pristine lake is home to the remarkable Idaho sockeye salmon.[12] As young fish, they travel a thousand miles to reach the Pacific Ocean, farther than any other North American salmon travel. There, the Idaho sockeye roam the Pacific for one to three years, feeding, gaining weight, and growing fast. Then, in midsummer, the fish start the thousand-mile journey back to their ancestral spawning ground. They swim back into the mountains, defying predators, defying obstacles, defying the dizzying 6,500-foot ascent up rivers and fast-moving mountain streams. Arriving back at Redfish Lake, the female sockeye will lay her eggs, often in the very same patch of lake-bed gravel where her life began.

Unlike many types of Atlantic salmon, Pacific salmon stop feeding once their homeward trek begins. Female sockeye will lose about 30 percent of their body weight by the time they reach natal waters—if they reach them at all.[13] Ragged, exhausted, fins disintegrating, the female lays her eggs in the gravel, covers them with her tail, and dies.

Most female sockeye die en route to the ocean or on the trip home. But whether they ultimately lay eggs or not, every sockeye contributes to its ecosystem. Predators such as bears gorge on the sudden glut of fish, storing up fat to survive the winter. The salmon's decaying bodies release a surge of nutrients into the comparatively sterile mountain water. In dying, the salmon make life possible for their own offspring (called fry) who feed on their remains. Dead salmon supply nutrients to Redfish Lake's animals and plants.

Idaho sockeye salmon are an example of what is known as a keystone species, meaning they influence the survival, or reproduction, of other species. Redfish Lake cannot thrive without the sockeye salmon, nor can the salmon survive without the resources in their ecosystem: open streams, spawning grounds, food for offspring.[14]

Water lilies are a keystone species in their ecosystem. The pond and its environs cannot survive without the lilies. Tadpoles find food and shelter in the lilies' shade. Tadpoles morph into frogs. Frogs sunbathe on the convenient lily pads. Snakes hunt frogs—and the cycle goes on.

This interdependence characterizes smart growth companies as well, companies that see themselves as an ecosystem with interdependent human elements, rather than disparate objects operating in isolation from one another, each tasked with its own exclusive routine. Apple understands this principle. Steve Jobs's genius lay in organizing the world's fifth largest corporation as if it were a small startup, where managers must cooperate laterally to overcome disagreements and stalemates. Managers don't get to operate in a bubble. None of Apple's divisional senior vice presidents (SVPs), for example, will oversee an Apple product start to finish. SVPs from different divisions must work together. Business sociologists Joel M. Podolny and Morten T. Hansen write that "the many horizontal dependencies mean that ineffective peer relationships . . . have the potential to undermine not only particular projects but the entire company. One bad apple really can spoil the bunch. Consequently, for people to attain and remain in a leadership position within a function, they must be highly effective collaborators."[15] In other words, succeeding in a top job at Apple requires cooperating—not competing—with peers and contributing to the ecosystem.

Keystone Species: You

I cannot underscore this truth enough: *We are responsible for making our own life decisions.* But we achieve very little by ourselves. There will always be people who help make us—whoever we become—possible. And, in my experience, the last person we think to thank is quite possibly the person who has helped us the most, the person we have taken most for granted as a constant—our water, our sunlight.

Just as you cannot grow without others, there are people who cannot grow without you. There are people for whom you are the keystone species. Are you contributing to a vicious or a virtuous growth cycle? Do you claim more than your share of resources—time, patience, energy, support—leaving a barren ecosystem for your fellow humans? Or are you generously contributing to the ecosystem? Are you a force for positive growth? The health of your ecosystem depends not only on what you get, but on what you give.

Joe DiSpenza, the *New York Times*–bestselling author who studies the neuroscience of change, reminds us, "Don't work on the relationship. Work on yourself, and the relationship [ecosystem] takes care of itself."[16] By "work on yourself," DiSpenza does not mean work exclusively in your own self-interest.

Let's look at the case of Erik Bursch, who in 2017 was a talented cloud-computing vice president at media and marketing giant Gannett Co., parent company of *USA Today*. Bursch led several critical tech and engineering teams in Gannett's technology division. He was advanced in his career. His teams were winning. But he felt that stagnant, I-could-do-this-job-in-my-sleep feeling we've encountered before. He'd maxed out his potential for learning and growth on his current S Curve and was bored and looking for a fresh challenge.

Getting a job at a different company would have been simple. His skills were in high demand. But Gannett felt like a friendly ecosystem to him; it felt like home. A good Explorer, he was looking for something with a substantial degree of familiarity but enough novelty to challenge him. His job was more than just a paycheck to him. Bursch wanted to help others grow as much as he wanted to grow himself.

He reached out to Jason Jedlinski, who was Gannett's SVP of consumer products at the time (today he has a similar role at the *Wall Street Journal*). Bursch proposed they combine their engineering teams. Internal mergers of this sort can generate a lot of counterproductive resentment and infighting, poisoning the ecosystem. But Jedlinski says that Bursch not only brought the best of his software development expertise to product development, he was also smart in his approach to people. Jedlinski said,

"[He] helped everyone level up in a way that wasn't arrogant; he didn't come in saying, *"You're going to do it my way.'* He took time to understand where his colleagues were in their growth." When leaders learn, their teams learn with them. "More than two dozen employees from this team were eventually promoted and we maintained one of the lowest attrition rates in the company," Jedlinski told me.

I asked Jedlinski how he created situations where growth happens, especially in a sensitive situation where divergent ecosystems are involved?

His answer: "First, help people understand how to successfully integrate." Bursch was already rooted in Gannett's ecosystem when he suggested they join forces, but company cultures have subcultures. The new team needed smart leadership and time to integrate. "Work to avoid cultural tissue rejection," Jedlinski told me. "Don't give pat advice [to incoming leaders], but specific, actionable intelligence. Second, respect the skills, experience, and insights [that Explorers like Bursch] bring to the table." For his part, Bursch says that it was mutual respect and shared goals that led to a series of platform and technical architecture innovations. He says, "It came from listening to our team, who organically came up with these ideas, saving hundreds of thousands of dollars while creating new strategic capabilities for the company."

In 2019, the GateHouse Media conglomerate acquired Gannett. In the aftermath of the acquisition, the team's innovative work saved scores of jobs when GateHouse selected Gannett's proprietary platform (some of the new strategic capabilities Bursch refers to) to power apps and websites for more than five hundred newspapers in forty-nine states. "[W]e were able to make a persuasive business case for our systems and our people," Jedlinski told me. Bursch was integral to that success. His smart growth leadership of the recently combined teams fostered collaboration rather than competition and resentment, stocking a pond where all could flourish. Jedlinski grew Bursch, Bursch grew their team members, and the team grew first Gannett and then GateHouse. These small, people-to-people ecosystems generate results far beyond their seemingly modest size.

There's a common cliché in corporate speak: *People are a company's greatest asset.* Not so fast, says Scott Miller. Miller is the former chief marketing officer at FranklinCovey, and the host of *On Leadership,* the world's largest leadership podcast. "It's the *relationships* between people that are a company's most valuable asset," says Miller. "You can copy everything: patents, logos, technology, supply chain, board of directors. What you cannot copy is how well people work together, how [they] defuse conflict, how they forgive each other, how skillsets complement deficiencies. People don't quit their jobs; they quit their bosses, they quit their cultures. They don't quit leaders who love them."[17]

Who needs you to be a smart growth parent, partner, coach, teacher, colleague, or manager?

Ed Catmull, cofounder of Pixar, created an ecosystem almost as famous as the studio's computer-animated films. He describes having basically stumbled into people management when he was seeking an opportunity to incorporate technology tools in movies. Essentially, he's a scientist. But Catmull was fascinated by fostering connection and cooperation between people, and studying how to build high-performing teams. This captured his imagination as much as emerging technologies did. Just as he aspired to give filmmakers technology tools, Catmull gave Pixar team members the psychological tools they needed to do great work. He focused on hiring skilled people who wanted to grow, but were hungry for an opportunity, rather than experts. He checked references, but didn't put new hires on probation. He instilled confidence by expressing confidence that they were equal to their responsibilities.

Catmull leads by believing people are worthy of his trust. He knows that trusting people fuels reciprocity—they trust him back, and it's natural to follow a leader we trust. On many occasions at Pixar, he says, he would share confidential things with individuals, and yet there was never a leak of sensitive information.

In the Pixar ecosystem under his leadership, employees felt connected to each other, unified in a common cause. They knew that their work mattered; but, even more, they mattered as human beings. That belief was forged during what Catmull describes as the "defining moment for the character of Pixar." Well along in the process of making *Toy Story II*, someone made a critical mistake, something as simple as pushing the wrong button. Backup procedures were inadequate, or perhaps weren't followed. It wasn't a technology failure; it was operator error. Perhaps several mistakes were made, and 90 percent of *Toy Story II* was lost. Thousands of hours of work were gone, except for what could be retrieved from the personal computer of an employee who'd been working from home on maternity leave.

Stunningly, there was no witch hunt for the responsible parties and culpability was never determined. "Accountability is something that we need to have, but it shouldn't be used as a weapon against people," he says. "And it often is." Catmull's message to his employees was that in Pixar's high character ecosystem, people were safe in making mistakes, and setbacks were expected. The work mattered, but his people mattered more. Perhaps because it renders so beautifully what we need from our ecosystem when we jump to a new S Curve, one of my favorite Pixar quotes is from the character Anton Ego, the food critic from one of Pixar's wonderful movies, *Ratatouille*. Ego could destroy restaurants with a single bad review and often delighted in doing so. Everyone feared him; no chef or maître d' wanted to see him at their door. Late in the film, a reformed Ego says,

> The work of a critic is easy. We risk little yet enjoy a position over those who offer up their work and themselves to our judgment. We thrive on negative criticism, which is fun to write and to read. The bitter truth we critics must face is that in the grand scheme of things, the average piece of junk is more meaningful than our criticism designating it so. But there are times when a critic truly risks something, and that is in the discovery and defense of the new. The world is often unkind to new talent, new creations. They need new friends.

It's not surprising that when I asked Catmull to approve the above excerpt for this book, he said to me, "Brad Bird (who also directed *The Incredibles*) gave voice to Anton Ego. These are his words. Is there a way to credit him?"[18] Like Hans Knoll before him, Catmull wants to give credit wherever and whenever possible.[19] Clayton Christensen once said, "If done well, management is the noblest of professions." Ed Catmull is a noble practitioner of the craft. He is a Creator of friendly environments, not a critic of people. Catmull helps others be smart about *their* growth.

Enriching the Ecosystem

In 1943, as World War II raged, the British House of Commons debated an important matter: architectural style.

During the Blitz earlier in the war, the Commons Chamber had been seriously damaged. Rebuilding it was a given, but hot debate centered on whether to do so in the old style. Some members wanted to change the "adversarial rectangular pattern" to the form of a semicircle or horseshoe design seen in some other legislative buildings, which was felt to foster a more cooperative spirit. Prime Minister Winston Churchill came down hard on the side of keeping the old design. Churchill insisted (a bit hyperbolically) that the shape of the old chamber was "responsible for the two-party system," which is the essence of British parliamentary democracy, famously claiming, "We shape our buildings, and afterwards our buildings shape us."[20]

I suspect Florence Knoll Bassett would have opposed Churchill's rebuild of the Commons Chamber on the old adversarial pattern. But she understood his point that a building is its own ecosystem; the form of the building informs the outlook of the people working in it. Perhaps when she sat down to create, she wanted us to feel something of what she had felt when she first saw the Kingswood School for Girls, a—twelve-year-old orphan alone in the world, walking through the front doors of a new home.

The connections between people are at least as critical to our growth as the relationships of roofline to wall to windows to floor are to the form and function of a building. We can work to design the human ecosystem purposefully and beautifully, so that it will inspire those who live and work in it. We can shape it to shape us. David Whyte, the Irish-English poet who you met in Metamorph (chapter 4), said that our legacy is embodied in what we leave behind, the "shape of our own absence."[21]

Like the water in the pond, or oxygen, or the sun (or even the snake), we all have a part to play in our ecosystem. We pull resources from our ecosystem to nourish ourselves. But our greatest legacy will be how we draw from our stores to help others grow. We must balance our take with our give, not depriving others, not poisoning the system. We must add sunshine. We must encourage young stems to grow.

As you join the convoys of your fellow S Curve travelers—some for a day, a few forever—what will you leave behind when you depart?

What will be the shape of your absence?

Ecosystem Takeaways

The S Curve of Learning sits within an ecosystem. This final chapter considers your place within the ecosystem where your growth happens. Our human tendency toward competition and independence hides the fact that our growth is entwined with the resources and relationships that surround and support us. The rate of growth and success you experience will flow directly from the wise cultivation of relationships and practical resources (for example, technology, tools) that comprise your ecosystem.

Relationships. Many of the important relationships in your life spring from environments you cannot choose, such as the family into which you were born or the friends you met in your first schools. As you become an autonomous adult, actively cultivate long-term relationships that can help you succeed along the S Curve. We—all of us—live, work, and grow in relation to other elements that can be purposefully organized.

What we need depends on where we are on the curve. Your ecosystem needs to provide different levels of support at different stages of the S Curve. You need support on the launch point: teachers, trainers, and mentors. In the sweet spot you need help to focus. You are going fast and feeling confident, but you still need people who are focused on you and can raise the red flag if your speed could lead to a crash. In the mastery stage, you need people who can celebrate with you and then give you a nudge to keep climbing.

Keystone species—you. Just as you cannot grow without others, there are people who cannot grow without you. You are their keystone species. Ask, "Am I contributing to a virtuous or a vicious growth cycle? Do I claim more than my share of resources—time, patience, energy, support—leaving a barren ecosystem for my fellow humans? Or am I generously contributing to this ecosystem? A force for positive growth?" The ecosystem you cultivate is about what you get and give.

. . .

As you travel the S Curve of life, your greatest legacy will be how you help others grow.

Ecosystem Summary for Smart Growth Leaders

Contribution is the sum of what grows when you are gone.

—TOM RATH

We are responsible for our own growth, but without a growth-friendly ecosystem little happens. Farmers monitor sunlight, water, and soil nutrients, and they control weeds and pests to maximize their crop yield. Similarly, when team leaders and organizations monitor their ecosystem for health, they can proactively direct team productivity.

In our research, we see that explicitly nurturing individual team members and positively and creatively approaching setbacks are uniquely important in helping people and organizations grow. Hence, this book. The data strongly suggest that teams provided with direct access to key decision makers have an ecosystem advantage. Conversely, even great team leaders can struggle when they are undermined by broader corporate systems.

Understand the current state of your team's biosphere: where your people are individually and collectively along the curve. Then you can identify where to invest resources to increase your yield.

Regardless of the size or type of your organization, the following series of exercises and questions—effectively a culture audit—will help you think about the ecosystem that you, as a manager, help create. In order to grow, every team member needs a culture that is healthy along these four dimensions: conducive, connected, resilient, and nurturing.

Conducive

To what extent does my team have the resources it needs?

Does the work environment motivate people to do their best work? Do they have the tools and training, and access to the right people? How does when and where they are required to work factor in? Do they have what they need to be effective?

Working with an executive at a *Fortune* 500 consumer products company, we identified that individuals on the launch point of their curves struggled for access to the people inside the organization from whom they needed help. This lowered the team's conducive score. Observe if people on the launch point in your organization face a similar challenge.

Make a prioritized list of the resources that would help your team flourish. Put a plan in place to secure them. Also, help the team see a shortage of resources as a tool of creation, an opportunity for innovation.[1]

Connective

How healthy are the relationships among the members of my team?

How clearly have I explained the connection between the work tasks of my team and the broad mission of my company?

Connectivity results when people feel as if they are seen at work, and that their manager cares about them. It also depends on whether people feel that they are contributing to the mission of your organization, that they are of useful service, and that they belong. Often the core issue is prioritizing communication. Clarify to your team and its constituent individuals how their efforts contribute to a larger cause. If you don't see the connection, address this with senior leadership. Perhaps they haven't clearly communicated how teams are contributing, or there is strategic misalignment needing attention.[2]

The relationships team members have with each other are their responsibility, but you have an important role to play. Model positive team conduct. When people onboard, include other people already on board in the process so they see their new colleagues as friends, not potential rivals. Enforce a zero-tolerance policy regarding gossip and backbiting. Require people to work together and publicly acknowledge them for healthy collaboration and team-work. Also be quick to apologize if you make a mistake, and quick to forgive others who apologize for their mistakes.

During a small group mastermind session with one of our clients, the CEO shared that a launch point executive made a misstep. Missteps frequently lead to disconnection, a feeling of not belonging. In this case the CEO reached out to the executive to say, "We are in this together." The mastermind discussion also involved a postmortem assessment by the two most senior executives on how they personally may have contributed to his misstep. They discussed precautions for the future. No gossiping, no undermining. Friends, not foes, working together in common cause. Unsurprisingly, the connective scores for this senior team are high.

Resilience

When mistakes happen, how and how often do they become opportunities to learn?

When there are setbacks—and there will be—what happens? Do you create an environment where constraints (for example, budgets and deadlines) are approached with positive motivation ("We'll figure this out") rather than sac-rificing quality to meet the deadline? Are mistakes an integral part of the pro-cess of growth and development, and do people talk openly about what worked and what didn't without blaming?

A CEO struggled with a major setback when the executive team discov-ered an oversight in the distribution process due to both the Covid-19 pan-demic and an ordering error. The oversight could set off a chain reaction from which it would be difficult to recover; the company could lose millions. After the team had pulled together to find an alternative distribution channel, the CEO assembled everyone for a postmortem that included celebrating an excellent strategic pivot. He emphasized his pride in the team's resilience in responding to this operational crisis, and supporting one another through per-sonal and family challenges.

Improve how your team responds to mistakes by reframing. Why did the failure occur? What process could be improved? Was it due to a lack of effort or trying something new? Is the person failing because they are in the wrong role? Are unrealistic expectations partly to blame? Failure is a constraint, but it can also be a tool of creation. Now that you've invested in this mistake, what will be your return-on-failure (ROF)?[3]

Resilience was pressure tested by the Covid-19 pandemic. We weren't surprised to see relatively low resilience scores for a number of teams we work with, and higher turnover. Monitoring resilience aids early recognition that to sustain momentum, an organization may need to provide more people support.

Nurturing

How well do I and my team encourage the growth of individual members?

Do the people who work with you feel that you care about their S Curve? This is not always easy to convey. Most of us are extremely task oriented. Tasks reduce anxiety. Think about how you plan your days. What if people, not tasks, were at the top of the list each day? What if every interaction was designed to develop the people that work with and for you?

Try this: make a list of all your direct reports. Then plan one day focused on helping the people on your team make progress. That is your only objective. See what happens.

When we support executives in facilitating off-sites, we emphasize the importance of the heads and tails of the interaction. Yes, the meat of the discussion—strategy and vision—is essential. But too often we start by leaving a discussion of people out of the lineup. All plants need water and sunlight, even the cactus. Put people, even the ones who don't need a lot, on the top of the list.

That, of course, is the crux of this book: grow yourself to grow your people to grow your company.

. . .

If you want to learn more about conducting a culture audit in your organization, go to disruptionadvisors.co/scurveplatform.

Epilogue

On such a full sea we are now afloat.

—WILLIAM SHAKESPEARE

When I moved from investment banking to equity research in 1997, the first stock I covered was a company called CIE (pronounced SEE-a), a concert promoter and venue operator in Latin America. My job was to build a financial model, evaluate the management team, and look for possible catalysts that would drive the stock up or down. All this would lead to an investment recommendation: buy, hold, or sell.

After months of due diligence, it was time to go public with my recommendation for CIE. The valuation looked reasonable, but the stock was up considerably. What if I rated CIE a "buy" and the price immediately dropped? There wasn't any obvious reason that it would go down, but afraid of looking foolish, I wanted to rate CIE "neutral": if you don't own, don't buy; if you do, don't sell. One colleague called me a shrinking violet. I own that. But then my boss, Jim Barrineau, prodded me, "Why wouldn't it keep going up?" CIE was beating its numbers and seemed to have momentum. Stocks go up based on what you expect (future), not on what they were (past). If you expect the numbers to be good, that's a growth stock. Barrineau asked why CIE wasn't a buy.

I stopped shrinking and started stretching. I put a buy on the stock. This experience was formative in my career. It taught me how to pick a stock, but it also led me to a far more personal question. Asking myself, "Why couldn't CIE keep going up?" eventually led to, "Do I believe I can keep growing?" This may seem like a nonintuitive leap, but that's what I do: I look for how ideas apply to me, and to you.

With Clayton Christensen's theory of disruptive innovation, I wondered how it might apply to people, which led to the framework of Personal Disruption. Studying E. M. Rogers's *Diffusion of Innovations* and his S Curve paradigm gradually brought me to the S Curve of Learning.

But before I worked with Christensen and before I knew about Rogers, my work on CIE led me to wonder why people can't be similar to a growth stock. As I grappled with a stock call that had the potential to put a sell on my career if I got it wrong, I asked myself the bigger question— *Can humans keep growing?*

It's been two decades since I put a buy on CIE, and my answer is that our human capacity for growth is unbounded.

Stocks often *do* keep going up, and we *can* continue to grow.

Some things grow without help or intervention. Some unwittingly choose not to grow. We become a worn-out water lily in an overgrown pond like our *Dear Abby* friend Mr. Blah, who we met in the introduction. But through the ebb and flow of life, growth remains the default setting for human beings.

Growth is not inscrutable. The process through which humans change and ultimately chart their own destiny can be analyzed and replicated.

The S Curve of Learning is the model.

The first time I read Rogers's *Diffusion of Innovations*, I encountered this quote from French sociologist Gabriel Tarde, written more than a hundred years ago: "A slow advance in the beginning, followed by rapid and uniformly accelerated progress, followed again by progress that continues to slacken until it finally stops: these are the three ages of invention. . . . If taken as a guide by the statistician and then by the sociologists, they would save many illusions."[1]

Applying Tarde's wisdom to smart growth, we recognize the three stages of the S Curve of Learning: the slow advance of the launch point, the rapid, accelerating progress of the sweet spot, the waning progress in mastery.

On virtually any learning curve, the finite resources for growth will eventually be used up, the limits of carrying capacity will be reached and exceeded. Potential for growth in that specific situation will be exhausted.

But for human beings, growth need not stop. Our growth can be exponential; the more we grow, the more we *can* grow. There is never really a conclusion; there are only new beginnings.

In my early school years, I learned that the earth has five oceans. I was growing up near the largest of these, the Pacific, which covers more than 30 percent of the planet, an area greater than the landmass of all the continents combined. The Atlantic is next in size, then the Indian, Southern (Antarctic), and Arctic oceans.

Later, I learned that oceans and seas aren't really the same thing; each ocean encompasses numerous seas—and straits and gulfs and bays. And later, still, I became aware that all this water can't really be demarcated in this way; the five oceans are really one great ocean of innumerable waves rolling continuously over almost three-quarters of the earth's surface, one into the next and then the next.

Every S Curve of Learning is a wave. Where there's one wave, there are many thousands, infinite in variety. We can only ride a fraction of them in this lifetime. We want to be smart, pick our waves—direct our own growth—then use our ever-expanding capacity to help others do the same.

As with our planet's single great ocean, there is one encompassing S Curve of Learning that is life, made up of contributing waves—a model for the human lifespan. At the launch point, we are infants, children, and adolescents. There is an enormous amount of learning to do, many mini-S Curve waves to master. By early adulthood, we have hopefully achieved a sufficient level of understanding and competence that we reach the tipping point of the life curve. Many years of productive work and valuable contributions follow—ideally, a lengthy prime of life spent scaling the exhilarating steep, sweet spot of our personal wave. Eventually, our progress slows as the wave of our life crests.

The S Curve of life, on inspection and introspection, is waves within waves within waves. Within the wave.

Notes

Introduction

1. Whitney Johnson, interview/personal correspondence with Astrid Tuminez, April 14, 2021, and *Disrupt Yourself* podcast, episode 232, September 7, 2021.

2. Whitney Johnson, "Disrupt Yourself," *Harvard Business Review*, July–August 2012, https://hbr.org/2012/07/disrupt-yourself-3.

3. Both *Disrupt Yourself* and *Build an A Team* articulate the framework of Personal Disruption with its seven accelerants of self reinvention. These accelerants are tools in your backpack that help you succeed on an S Curve journey. For more on the Personal Disruption framework, listen to the *Disrupt Yourself* podcast, Episode 80, "Disrupt Yourself Today."

4. Everett M. Rogers, ed., *Diffusion of Innovations*, 5th ed. (New York: Free Press, 2003), 13.

5. Whitney Johnson, "Throw Your Life a Curve," hbr.org, September 3, 2012, https://hbr.org/2012/09/throw-your-life-a-curve.

6. The S Curve Insight Platform tracks the progress of individuals and teams, the tools being used to accelerate their progress, and generates insights on how to accelerate organizational growth. For further information, go to disruptionadvisors.co/scurveplatform.

7. Whitney Johnson, interview with Harry Kraemer, *Disrupt Yourself* podcast, episode 236, October 5, 2021.

8. Bruce Japsen, "CEO Steps Up, Takes Blame," *Chicago Tribune*, January 30, 2004, https://www.chicagotribune.com/news/ct-xpm-2004-01-30-0401300327-story.html.

9. Abigail Van Buren, "Dear Abby: Teen Tells Mom to Stay Away During His Band Performances," *Bowling Green Daily News*, June 16, 2017, https://www.bgdailynews.com/community/dear-abby-teen-tells-mom-to-stay-away-during-his/article_bbbe40c4-f871-561e-9034-f749e755dc25.html.

S Curve Implications for Smart Growth Leaders

1. The Platform helps answer questions such as: Are my strongest performers potentially bored, do they need a new challenge, are they considering leaving? Which areas of the organization have a surplus of strong performers approaching mastery who could be redeployed? Where are we overindexed with people on the launch point? The platform also identifies culture hot spots—departments (and managers) where growth is happening. For further information, go to disruptionadvisors.co/scurveplatform.

Chapter 1: Explorer

1. Shakespeare is speaking through Brutus in *Julius Caesar*. Brutus is indulging in hyperbole. We are not fated for either happiness or misery, and our lives will offer many opportunities full of fortune. Given that Brutus chose the course that ended on his own sword, maybe he doesn't know everything.

2. Whitney Johnson, interview with Mike Rowe, *Disrupt Yourself* podcast, episode 231, August 31, 2021.

3. "What to Do When There Are Too Many Product Choices on the Store Shelves?," *Consumer Reports*, January 2014, https://www.consumerreports.org/cro/magazine/2014/03/too-many-product-choices-in-supermarkets/index.htm.

4. Nicole Spector, "Why Our Sense of Time Speeds Up as We Age—and How to Slow It Down," NBC News/Today, November 26, 2018, https://www.nbcnews.com/better/health/why-our-sense-time-speeds-we-age-how-slow-it-ncna936351.

5. In 1997, clinical psychologist James Prochaska identified five distinct stages for significant personal change. Prochaska studies the changes individuals must make to lower their risk of cancer and diabetes. Prochaska's theory posits that those who achieve lasting change generally pass through five stages: 1) precontemplation; 2) contemplation; 3) preparation; 4) action; and 5) maintenance. Prochaska graphs these stages along an S-shaped curve, with slow progress at the base (precontemplation; contemplation), acceleration in the middle (preparation; action), and mastery at the peak (maintenance).

Prochaska teaches that those who achieve significant personal change start at the slow phase of precontemplation. "Contemplation," Prochaska writes, "is the stage in which people are intending to change in the next six months. They are more aware of the pros of changing but are also acutely aware of the cons." Hello, Explorers.

For more information see University of Rhode Island Cancer Prevention Research Center, "Detailed Overview: Transtheoretical Model of Change," https://web.uri.edu/cprc/detailed-overview.

6. Whitney Johnson, interview with Marco Trecroce, "Take Time to Plan," *Disrupt Yourself* podcast, episode 150, February 25, 2020, https://whitneyjohnson.com/marco-trecroce/.

7. Neville Goddard, *The Power of Awareness* (Seattle, WA: Pacific Publishing Studio, 2010), 54.

8. Whitney Johnson, interview with Marcus Whitney, "Create and Orchestrate," *Disrupt Yourself* podcast, episode 188, November 3, 2020, https://whitneyjohnson.com/marcus-whitney/.

9. Marcus Whitney, *Create and Orchestrate: The Path to Claiming Your Creative Power from an Unlikely Entrepreneur* (self-pub., Creative Power, 2020), 39.

10. For more on this topic, listen to Whitney Johnson, interview with Bob Proctor, "Change Your Paradigm, Change Your Life," *Disrupt Yourself* podcast, episode 208, March 23, 2021, https://whitneyjohnson.com/bob-proctor/.

11. Thank you to James Clear for inspiring this process. Whitney Johnson, interview with James Clear, "Just One Percent Better," *Disrupt Yourself* podcast, episode 93, January 15, 2019, https://whitneyjohnson.com/james-clear/ and "Atomic Habits: Encore Episode," *Disrupt Yourself* podcast, episode 190, November 17, 2020, https://whitneyjohnson.com/james-clear-encore/.

12. Whitney Johnson, interview with Darrell Rigby, "The Agile Life," *Disrupt Yourself* podcast, episode 176, August 11, 2020, https://whitneyjohnson.com/darrell-rigby/.

13. Agile methods or agile processes generally promote a disciplined project management process that encourages frequent inspection and adaptation, a leadership philosophy that encourages teamwork, self-organization, and accountability.

14. Darrell Rigby, Sarah Elk, and Steve Berez, *Doing Agile Right: Transformation without Chaos* (Boston: Harvard Business Review Press, 2020).

15. Whitney Johnson, interview with Rita McGrath, "Inflection Points," *Disrupt Yourself* podcast, episode 126, September 3, 2019, https://whitneyjohnson.com/rita-mcgrath/.

16. Queens University, "Discovery of 'Thought Worms' Opens Window to the Mind," Neuroscience News.com, July 14, 2020, https://neurosciencenews.com/thought-worms-16639/.

17. Whitney Johnson, interview with Tara Swart, "Unlock Your Mind and Reach Your Potential," *Disrupt Yourself* podcast, episode 156, March 27, 2020.

18. Brian Uzzi et al., "Atypical Combinations and Scientific Impact," *Science* 342, no. 6257 (2013): 468–472.

19. Derek Thompson, *Hit Makers: How to Succeed in the Age of Distraction* (New York: Penguin, 2017), 79.

20. Whitney Johnson, interview with Jamie O'Banion and Melbourne O'Banion, "In Good Company," *Disrupt Yourself* podcast, episode 203, February 16, 2021, https://whitneyjohnson.com/jamie-melbourne-obanion/ and conversation with the author, March 29, 2021.

21. Clayton M. Christensen, James Allworth, and Karen Dillon, *How Will You Measure Your Life?* (New York: Harper Collins, 2012), 203–204.

22. Whitney Johnson, interview with Angela Blanchard, "The Measure of a Great City," *Disrupt Yourself* podcast, episode 146, January 28, 2020, https://whitneyjohnson.com/angela-blanchard/.

23. For more on my foundational assumptions for this book, see disruptionadvisors.co/smartgrowthbook.

24. For more on shadow values, go to www.disruptionadvisors.co/smartgrowthbook.

25. Dartmouth University, "2015 Commencement Address by David Brooks," June 14, 2015, https://news.dartmouth.edu/news/2015/06/2015-commencement-address-david-brooks.

26. Simon Sinek, "Friends Exercise," accessed July 13, 2021, https://simonsinek.com/commit/test-your-why/.

Chapter 2: Collector

1. Whitney Johnson, interview with Mikaila Ulmer, "Bee Fearless," *Disrupt Yourself* podcast, episode 182, September 22, 2020, https://whitneyjohnson.com/mikaila-ulmer/.

2. Christopher Ingraham, "Call Off the Bee-pocalypse: U.S. Honeybee Colonies Hit a 20-Year High," *Washington Post*, June 23, 2015, https://www.washingtonpost.com/news/wonk/wp/2015/07/23/call-off-the-bee-pocalypse-u-s-honeybee-colonies-hit-a-20-year-high/.

3. Kiki Schockling, "Data in Everyday Life: Are Honey Bees on the Decline?," PQ Systems, May 14, 2019, https://blog.pqsystems.com/2019/05/14/data-in-everyday-life-are-honey-bees-on-the-decline/.

4. We always court the risk of sunk costs, luring us to continue to pursue something because we've already begun. It's hard to pull the plug and lose our investment of time. Confirmation bias, the tendency to interpret new information as confirmation of what we already believe, is another lurking risk.

5. Carol S. Dweck, *Mindset: The New Psychology of Success* (New York: Ballantine Books, 2007).

6. Zachary Crockett, "Shark Tank Deep Dive: A Data Analysis of All 10 Seasons," The Hustle, May 19, 2019, https://thehustle.co/shark-tank-data-analysis-10-seasons/.

7. Apple Montessori Schools, "Our Favorite Montessori Quotes," https://www.applemontessorischools.com/montessori-quotes.

8. Joyce Sidman, *The Girl Who Drew Butterflies: How Maria Merian's Art Changed Science* (Boston, New York: Houghton Mifflin Harcourt, 2018).

9. Max Roser and Estaban Ortiz-Ospina, "Literacy," Our World in Data, 2013, revised September 20, 2018, https://ourworldindata.org/literacy.

10. Amanda Vickery, "Flora, Fauna and Fortitude: The Extraordinary Mission of Maria Sibylla Merian," *Guardian*, April 1, 2016, www.theguardian.com/artanddesign/2016/apr/01/flora-fauna-and-fortitude-the-extraordinary-mission-of-maria-sibylla-merian.

11. Assuming there are sufficient resources for lilies to begin life in this pond, the lilies' proliferation rate will actually be highest at the outset. In terms of the percentage of overall change (e.g., the percentage of growth between .5 and 1 is greater (100%) than that between 2 and 3 (50%), even though the actual gap between the latter two is greater). This is a metaphor for what happens at the launch point of the S Curve. Growth may not be evident, but below detection, considerable progress is underway. For more on the math, see www.disruptionadvisors.co/smartgrowthbook.

12. A third book, *Let's Learn Our Way Through It, Shall We?*, chronicles her early years as chief learning and diversity officer at Kraft Heinz.

13. Tara Swart, *The Source: The Secrets of the Universe, the Science of the Brain* (New York: HarperOne, 2019), 195.

14. Daniel Goleman, *Focus: The Hidden Driver of Excellence* (New York: Harper, 2015), 2.

15. Rosabeth Moss Kanter, "Managing Yourself: Zoom In and Zoom Out," *Harvard Business Review*, March 2011, https://hbr.org/2011/03/managing-yourself-zoom-in-zoom-out.

16. Loren W. Christensen and Dave Grossman, *On Combat: The Psychology and Physiology of Deadly Conflict in War and in Peace* (self-pub., Warrior Science Publications, 2008).

17. Whitney Johnson, interview with Scott Pulsipher, "Disruptive Leadership in Higher Education," *Disrupt Yourself* podcast, episode 32, November 2, 2017, https://whitney johnson.com/scott-pulsipher/.

18. For more on Play to Your Strengths, listen to Whitney Johnson, "Play to Your Disctinctive Strengths," *Disrupt Yourself* podcast, episode 120, July 23, 2019, https://whitneyjohnson.com/distinctive-strengths/.

19. Whitney Johnson, interview with Sandy Stelling, "The Language of Growth," *Disrupt Yourself* podcast, December 8, 2020, https://whitneyjohnson.com/sandy-stelling/.

20. Gregory M. Walton, "The New Science of Wise Psychological Interventions," *Current Directions in Psychological Science* 23, no. 1 (2014): 74.

21. Whitney Johnson, interview with Eric Schurenberg, "Be Discovery Driven," *Disrupt Yourself* podcast, episode 135, November 5, 2019, https://whitneyjohnson.com/eric -schurenberg/, and follow-up conversation.

22. Private correspondence with author.

Part 1: Launch Point for Smart Growth Leaders

1. Conversation with the author, May 17, 2021.

2. The S Curve Insight Platform tracks and monitors individual and collective progress. It informs talent development/retention/workforce and succession planning. (For further information, go to disruptionadvisors.co/scurveplatform.)

Chapter 3: Accelerator

1. Dr. Sejnowski and I were discussing his much-cited experiment, wherein Sejnowski and his colleagues at the Salk Institute for Biological Studies compared the brains of wild mice to the brains of mice raised in captivity. Sejnowski observed that "when mice are in the wild, where they can run and explore and acquire some stress, new neurons are born in order to survive." The robust lifestyle of wild mice accelerates the synaptic uptake of fresh neurons into the animals' brains. A physicist turned biologist, Sejnowski himself is no stranger to new S Curves. See Henriette van Praag et al., "Running Enhances Neurogenesis, Learning, and Long-Term Potentiation in Mice," *PNAS* 96, no. 23 (1999): 13427–13431.

2. Whitney Johnson, interview with Jeremy Andrus, "Building Something of Value," *Disrupt Yourself* podcast, episode 148, February 11, 2020, https://whitneyjohnson.com /jeremy-andrus/.

3. Aisley Oliphant, "CEO of the Year," *Utah Business*, April 4, 2016, https://www .utahbusiness.com/ceo-of-the-year/.

4. Johnson, interview with Jeremy Andrus.

5. Wikipedia, "Saturn V," https://en.wikipedia.org/wiki/Saturn_V.

6. Self-determination is a psychological concept referring to an individual's "ability to make choices and manage their own life." It impacts mental health, well-being, and motivation. See https://www.verywellmind.com/what-is-self-determination-theory -2795387.

7. "The Traeger story is now aimed squarely at foodies and outdoor-loving Gen X-ers and Millennials," wrote TechCrunch. See John Biggs, "Traeger's Wi-Fi Connected

Grill Is Delicious Overkill," TechCrunch, February 12, 2018, https://techcrunch.com/2018/02/12/traegers-wi-fi-connected-grill-is-delicious-overkill/.

8. Whitney Johnson, interview/personal correspondence with Astrid Tuminez, April 14, 2021, and Whitney Johnson, *Disrupt Yourself* podcast, episode 232, September 7, 2021.

9. Astrid's wealth of human resources underscores the importance of relatedness, which we'll talk about in a moment.

10. Whitney Johnson, interview with Liz O'Donnell, "Stepping Back and Showing Up," *Disrupt Yourself* podcast, episode 168, June 16, 2020, https://whitneyjohnson.com/liz-odonnell/.

11. Anand Mahindra, *Change the Rules* (New Delhi: Penguin Petit, 2015), 7.

12. Priyanka B. Carr and Gregory M. Walton, "Cues of Working Together Fuel Intrinsic Motivation," *Journal of Experimental Social Psychology* 53 (2014): 169–184.

13. See also Heidi Grant, "Managers Can Motivate Employees with One Word," hbr.org, August 13, 2014, https://hbr.org/2014/08/managers-can-motivate-employees-with-one-word.

14. Whitney Johnson, interview with Zaza Pachulia, "The Game of Disruption," *Disrupt Yourself* podcast, episode 183, September 29, 2020, https://whitneyjohnson.com/zaza-pachulia/.

15. Devin Kharpertian, "ESPN's Thorpe Rips Kidd: 'He's the Worst Coach in the NBA'," Brooklyn Game, November 15, 2013, http://thebrooklyngame.com/espns-thorpe-rips-kidd-hes-the-worst-coach-in-the-nba/.

16. Roy Baumeister and Mark Leary, "The Need to Belong: Desire for Personal Attachments as a Fundamental Human Motivation," *Psychological Bulletin* 117, no. 3 (1995): 497–529.

17. Whitney Johnson, interview with Donna Hicks, "Guardians of Dignity," *Disrupt Yourself* podcast, episode 92, January 8, 2019, https://whitneyjohnson.com/donna-hicks/.

18. "Warriors Capture Second-Straight NBA Championship," NBA.com, June 8, 2018, https://www.nba.com/warriors/gameday/20180608/recap.

19. David Rock, *Your Brain at Work: Strategies for Overcoming Distraction, Regaining Focus, and Working Smarter All Day Long* (New York: Harper Business, 2020), 167.

20. Relatedness is so important to our growth from launch point to mastery that we have an entire chapter largely devoted to this topic—Ecosystem, chapter 7.

21. A compounded return means that you earn interest not just on your initial investment but also on the accumulated returns on that investment. In this example, during the second year you would earn interest not only on the initial $100 invested, but on $105, the initial investment plus the $5 interest earned in year one.

22. Myron Scholes, "A R(evolution) in Asset Management," YouTube video, posted November 15, 2017, https://www.youtube.com/watch?v=nxKlnsX8DS4.

23. Whitney Johnson, *Build an A Team: Play to Their Strengths and Lead Them Up the Learning Curve* (Boston: Harvard Business Review Press, 2018), 18.

24. If, like me, you find yourself on the launch point of being able to pronounce his name, here's the phonetic guide: muh-HAY-lee cheek-sent-me-HIGH-lee.

25. Mihaly Csikszentmihalyi, *Flow: The Psychology of Optimal Experience* (New York: HarperCollins, 2008), 10.

Chapter 4: Metamorph

1. Whitney Johnson, interview with Michelle McKenna, "Change Agents," *Disrupt Yourself* podcast, episode 172, July 14, 2020, https://whitneyjohnson.com/michelle-mckenna/. See also episode 1, "Disrupting the NFL," September 23, 2016, https://whitneyjohnson.com/michelle-mckenna-doyle-disrupt-yourself/. Michelle was the very first guest on the *Disrupt Yourself* podcast.

2. John Breech, "NFL Coronavirus Fallout: League Is Requiring Employees to Work from Home; Free Agency Still Starting on Time," CBS, March 12, 2020, https://www

.cbssports.com/nfl/news/nfl-coronavirus-fallout-league-is-requiring-employees-to-work
-from-home-will-free-agency-be-delayed/.

3. Hanna Inam, interview with Richard Boyatzis, "What Neuroscience Can Teach Us About Being Agile to Change," *Transformational Leadership* podcast, episode 5, May 4, 2020, https://transformleaders.tv/richard-boyatzis/.

4. Since Csikszentmihalyi wrote this in the 90s, I am going to extrapolate that this would include any kind of passively consumed media. Mihaly Csikszentmihalyi, *Flow: The Psychology of Optimal Experience* (New York: Harper Perennial Modern Classics, 2008), 83.

5. Jason Dachman, "NFL Draft 2020: NFL Media Deploys iPhone Production Kits, Coordinates 600+ Live Feeds to Bring Virtual Draft to Fans," SVG News, April 23, 2020, https://www.sportsvideo.org/2020/04/23/nfl-draft-2020-nfl-media-deploys-iphone
-production-kits-coordinates-600-live-feeds-to-bring-virtual-draft-to-fans/.

6. Alvin Powell, "Ellen Langer's State of Mindfulness," *Harvard Gazette*, October 1, 2018, https://news.harvard.edu/gazette/story/2018/10/ellen-langer-talks-mindfulness-health/.

7. Emma McAdam, Therapy in a Nutshell, "How to Turn Off the Fear Response: Create a Sense of Safety," YouTube video, posted on April 27, 2021, https://www.youtube
.com/watch?v=0DpDywOxEWc&t=300s.

8. Whitney Johnson, interview with Shawn Stevenson, "Eat Smarter," *Disrupt Yourself* podcast, episode 202, February 9, 2021, https://whitneyjohnson.com/shawn-stevenson/.

9. Barbara Oakley, *Mindshift: Break Through Obstacles to Learning and Discover Your Hidden Potential* (New York: TarcherPerigee, 2017), 34; and Joseph Cichon, "Sleep Promotes Branch-Specific Formation of Dendritic Spines after Learning," Neuroscience Institute Journal Club, 2014, https://med.nyu.edu/departments-institutes/neuroscience
/research/journal-club/journal-club-2014-articles/sleep-promotes-branch-specific
-formation-dendritic-spines-learning.

10. Henriette van Praag et al., "Running Enhances Neurogenesis, Learning, and Long-Term Potentiation in Mice," *PNAS* 96, no. 23 (1999): 13427–13431.

11. Author correspondence with Sejnowski.

12. Whitney Johnson, interview with Ryan Westwood, "The Power of Partnering," *Disrupt Yourself* podcast, episode 192, December 1, 2020, https://whitneyjohnson.com
/ryan-westwood/.

13. Ryan Westwood, "Three Lessons Learned from a High Growth Tech CEO," *Forbes*, February 11, 2015, https://www.forbes.com/sites/ryanwestwood/2015/02/11/three
-lessons-learned-from-a-high-growth-tech-ceo/?sh=634f995150b1.

14. Westwood coauthored *Five Secrets of Successful Entrepreneurs* in 2011.

15. Rollo May, *The Courage to Create* (New York: W.W. Norton, 1994), 112.

16. May, *Courage to Create*, 113.

17. Francesca Gino, "Are You Too Stressed to Be Productive? Or Not Stressed Enough?," hbr.org, April 14, 2016, https://hbr.org/2016/04/are-you-too-stressed-to-be
-productive-or-not-stressed-enough.

18. Yale School of Medicine, "The Inverted U-Alterations in PFC Function Based on Arousal State," https://medicine.yale.edu/lab/arnsten/research/invertedu/.

19. Krista Tippett, interview with David Whyte, "The Conversational Nature of Reality," *On Being with Krista Tippett*, April 7, 2016, https://onbeing.org/programs/david
-whyte-the-conversational-nature-of-reality/#transcript.

20. Eugene P. Kiver and David V. Harris, *Geology of U.S. Parklands*, 5th edition (John Wiley & Sons, 1999), 523.

Part 2: Sweet Spot for Smart Growth Leaders

1. Procurious, "Alan Mulally—the Secret to Success in One Slide," May 31, 2016, https://www.procurious.com/procurement-news/alan-mulally-secret-success.

2. The S Curve Insight Platform tracks and monitors individual and collective progress. It informs talent development/retention/workforce and succession planning. For further information, go to disruptionadvisors.co/scurveplatform.

Chapter 5: Anchor

1. All quotes are either from Whitney Johnson, interview with Erik and Emily Orton, "Failing Forward, Failing Better," *Disrupt Yourself* podcast, episode 101, March 12, 2019, https://whitneyjohnson.com/erik-emily-orton; or from Erik Orton and Emily Orton, *Seven at Sea: Why a New York City Family Cast Off Convention for a Life-Changing Year on a Sailboat* (Salt Lake City, UT: Shadow Mountain, 2019).

2. Named after Fezziwig, the good-natured, generous counterpoint to Ebenezer Scrooge in Charles Dickens's *A Christmas Carol.*

3. There were other consequential considerations, such as personal safety, especially for their young children. They mitigated risk with strict rules about wearing life jackets and being attached to the boat by a jackline. As they grew more competent, some of the rules were eased, but they were always careful about monitoring the weather to avoid sailing in storms.

4. Frank E. Manning, ed., *The Celebration of Society: Perspectives on Contemporary Cultural Performance* (Bowling Green, OH: Bowling Green State University, 1983).

5. Whitney Johnson, interview with Harry Kraemer, *Disrupt Yourself* podcast, episode 236, October 5, 2021.

6. B. J. Fogg, "How You Can Use the Power of Celebration to Make New Habits," TED, January 6, 2020, https://ideas.ted.com/how-you-can-use-the-power-of-celebration-to-make-new-habits-stick/. If interested, he was also on the *Disrupt Yourself* podcast, "Creating Tiny Habits," episode 145, January 21, 2020, https://whitneyjohnson.com/bj-fogg/.

7. Sometimes known by the shorthand "Mormon," the official name is The Church of Jesus Christ of Latter-day Saints.

8. Librettists compose the lyrics to long vocal works such as operas, musicals, and song cycles.

9. Center for Latter-day Saint Arts, https://www.centerforlatterdaysaintarts.org/create-lesson-a-teensadults.

10. Interview with author, September 23, 2020.

11. Fred B. Bryant and Joseph Verhoff, *Savoring: A New Model of Positive Experience* (London: Psychology Press, 2006), 33–34.

12. Dan Pink, *When: The Scientific Secrets of Perfect Timing* (Melbourne: Text Publishing, 2018), 164.

13. Whitney Johnson, interview with Zaza Pachulia, "The Game of Disruption," *Disrupt Yourself* podcast, episode 183, September 29, 2020, https://whitneyjohnson.com/zaza-pachulia/.

14. Immigration has been a blessing for some and a curse for others. Four hundred years of migration to the United States, for example, has resulted in the displacement and marginalization of many people here, including the native population. I acknowledge that the history of immigration is complex, and hardly an unmitigated success story, morally or otherwise. Immigration is, however, an arduous S Curve that invites study for its lessons on learning and growth.

15. "Immigration and Emigration," Legacies BBC, http://www.bbc.co.uk/legacies/immig_emig/england/cornwall/article_3.shtml.

16. Lauren Cocking, "A Piece of Britain Lost in Mexico," BBC Travel, May 21, 2018, http://www.bbc.com/travel/story/20180520-a-piece-of-britain-lost-in-mexico.

17. Samuel Turner, "The Cornish Miners Who Brought Football to Mexico," *Falmouth Anchor*, October 20, 2018, http://www.falmouth-anchor.co.uk/2018/10/20/the-cornish-miners-who-brought-football-to-mexico/.

18. Recorded interview, January 20, 2021.

Chapter 6: Mountaineer

1. Hewlett-Packard Journal, June 1989, https://www.hpl.hp.com/hpjournal/pdfs/IssuePDFs/1989-06.pdf.

2. Whitney Johnson, interview with Feyzi Fatehi, "Scaling Personal and Professional Summits," *Disrupt Yourself* podcast, episode 28, October 5, 2017, https://whitneyjohnson.com/feyzi-fatehi/.

3. Whitney Johnson, interview with Tara Swart, "Unlock Your Mind and Reach Your Potential," *Disrupt Yourself* podcast, episode 156, March 27, 2020, https://whitneyjohnson.com/tara-swart/.

4. Daniel Wolpert, "The Real Reason for Brains," TEDGlobal 2011, https://www.ted.com/talks/daniel_wolpert_the_real_reason_for_brains/transcript?language=en.

5. About her book *The Source*, Deepak Chopra said that Swart's achievement lies in "[marrying] universal truths with scientific rigor."

6. To close the open loop, the most influential was John Thompson, then CEO of Virtual Instruments, former chairman of the board at Microsoft, and now a venture partner at Lightspeed Venture Partners.

7. Whitney Johnson, interview with Shellye Archambeau, "Unapologetically Ambitious," *Disrupt Yourself* podcast, episode 184, October 6, 2020, https://whitneyjohnson.com/shellye-archambeau/.

8. Hilary Brueck, "Dead Bodies Litter Mount Everest Because It's So Dangerous and Expensive to Get Them Down," *Business Insider*, May 28, 2019, https://www.businessinsider.com/dead-bodies-on-mount-everest-are-hard-to-get-down-2019-5.

9. In his book *Behavioral and Neural Plasticity*, Michael M. Nikoletseas teaches that habituation is an organism's decremented response to environmental stimuli that it experiences repeatedly over time. Habituation leads to a behavioral plateau, where the organism responds minimally, if at all, to events that it has found to be predictable. Nikoletseas writes that "if we present a stimulus many times, the organism will either stop responding, or respond minimally at a lower level. Eventually, no matter how many more times we present the stimulus, we do not see any further change. The curve plateaus, we say." Nikoletseas notes that humans will also exhibit decremented responses to events that have become all too familiar. In essence, the individual has reached the point where they learn nothing more than a reflexive response to the event: neural rigidity in action. Michael M. Nikoletseas, *Behavioral and Neural Plasticity* (CreateSpace Independent Publishing, 2010), 42.

10. James M. Citrin, Claudius A. Hildebrand, and Robert J. Stark, "The CEO Life Cycle," *Harvard Business Review*, November–December 2019.

11. Don J. Snyder, *The Cliff Walk: A Memoir of a Job Lost and a Life Found* (New York: Little, Brown, 1997).

12. Snyder, *The Cliff Walk*, 199–200.

13. I'm impressed by Snyder's keen look at America's pro white-collar bias. To echo one of Snyder's advance reviewers, "The housebuilding section contains some of the best writing about work in American literature."

14. Whitney Johnson, interview with Bettina Hein and Andreas Goeldi, "Dynamic Duo," *Disrupt Yourself* podcast, episode 191, November 24, 2020, https://whitneyjohnson.com/bettinahein-andreasgoeldi/.

15. She speaks from experience. She is a serial venture-backed entrepreneur, founder, and former CEO of the US-based software company Pixability. Hein also cofounded SVOX: a Swiss language technology company that ultimately sold for $125 million. Currently CEO of her 2020 startup, Juli Health, Hein's data-analysis prototype helps subscribers manage chronic health conditions via an AI-powered app: the cutting edge of digital health care. But the Swiss are more likely to recognize Hein as one of the keen-minded investors on *Die Höhle der Löwen*—"the lion's den"—Switzerland's answer to *Shark Tank*.

Part 3: Mastery for Smart Growth Leaders

1. The S Curve Insight Platform tracks and monitors individual and collective progress. It informs talent development/retention/workforce and succession planning. For further information, go to disruptionadvisors.co/scurveplatform.

2. For more on how managers encourage new S Curves, listen to Whitney Johnson, interview with Scott O'Neil, "Connect, Be Present, Dream Bigger," *Disrupt Yourself* podcast, episode 219, June 8, 2021, https://whitneyjohnson.com/219-scott-oneil/.

3. The S Curve Insight Platform tracks and monitors individual and collective progress. It informs talent development/retention/workforce and succession planning. For further information, go to disruptionadvisors.co/scurveplatform.

Chapter 7: Ecosystem

1. Robert D. McFadden, "Florence Knoll Bassett, 101, Designer of the Modern American Office, Dies," *New York Times*, January 25, 2019, https://www.nytimes.com/2019/01/25/style/florence-knoll-bassett-dead.html.

2. Knoll, "Florence Knoll Bassett, Design Pioneer and Guiding Light of Knoll, Dies at 101," https://www.knoll.com/knollnewsdetail/florence-knoll-bassett-dies-at-101.

3. Knoll Designer Bios, "Florence Knoll," https://www.knoll.com/designer/Florence-Knoll.

4. Maria Popova, *Figuring* (New York: Pantheon Books, 2019).

5. Kathleen Elkins, "Warren Buffett and Sheryl Sandberg Agree on the Most Important Decision You Will Ever Make," CNBC, February 7, 2017, https://www.cnbc.com/2017/02/07/warren-buffett-and-sheryl-sandberg-agree-on-most-important-decision.html.

6. Elkins, "Warren Buffett and Sheryl Sandberg Agree."

7. Today's designers commonly borrow KPU's signature cardboard mockup—known as a "paste-up"—when presenting different design options to their clients. Florence also established Knoll Textiles, and with it the practice of attaching small swatches of fabric to her models for clients to see and choose from. Knoll Associates developed a reputation for superlative modern design, and Florence invited her former mentors and teachers—including her close friend Eero Saarinen—to design cutting-edge furniture pieces for the business. Saarinen's iconic Womb Chair and Tulip Table and Chair, commissioned by Florence for Knoll, are still considered icons of midcentury modern design.

8. Knoll, "Hans Knoll Centennial," https://www.knoll.com/knollnewsdetail/happy-birthday-hans-knoll.

9. Melinda Blau and Karen Fingerman, *Consequential Strangers: Turning Everyday Encounters into Life-Changing Moments* (New York: W.W. Norton, 2010), 30.

10. This technique has helped other entertainers as well, notably James Earl Jones.

11. Whitney Johnson, interview with Harry Kraemer, *Disrupt Yourself* podcast, episode 236, October 5, 2021.

12. Sawtooth Interpretive and Historical Association, "What Happened to the Red Fish of Redfish Lake," July 24, 2020, https://discoversawtooth.org/what-happened-to-the-red-fish-of-redfish-lake.

13. Joseph R. Burger et al., "Metabolic Life Tables: The Sockeye Salmon Example," https://doi.org/10.1101/2020.03.13.990986.

14. There are several lakes in the vicinity of Redfish Lake that were once home to abundant salmon populations. No more. Idaho sockeye salmon are an endangered species. Humans are disrupting the sockeye in a variety of ways, most of all with the seven major dams the fish encounter between the Pacific Ocean and Redfish Lake. And it isn't just a problem for the salmon. Without the decaying bodies of the mature fish, most other forms of life are disappearing from the lake as well. It is becoming a sterile ecosystem.

15. Joel M. Podolny and Morten T. Hansen, "How Apple Is Organized for Innovation," *Harvard Business Review*, November–December 2020, https://hbr.org/2020/11/how-apple-is-organized-for-innovation.

16. Joe Dispenza, "How to Unlock the Full Potential of Your Mind," YouTube video, posted June 12, 2018, https://www.youtube.com/watch?v=La9oLLoI5Rc.

17. Whitney Johnson, interview with Scott Miller, "Becoming the Leader People Want to Follow," *Disrupt Yourself* podcast, episode 154, March 19, 2020, https://whitneyjohnson.com/scott-miller/.

18. Whitney Johnson, interview with Ed Catmull, "Marvelous Moments," *Disrupt Yourself* podcast, episode 210, April 6, 2021, https://whitneyjohnson.com/ed-catmull/.

19. To learn from another ecosystem creator, listen to Whitney Johnson, interview with Justin Osofsky, "Insight from Instagram," *Disrupt Yourself* podcast, episode 218, June 1, 2021, https://whitneyjohnson.com/218-justin_osofsky-insight-from-instagram/.

20. UK Parliament, "Churchill and the Commons Chamber," https://www.parliament.uk/about/living-heritage/building/palace/architecture/palacestructure/churchill/.

21. Andy Walton, "The Shape of Absence," *One Eternal Presence* (blog), April 13, 2016, http://oneeternalpresence.blogspot.com/2016/04/the-shape-of-absence.html.

Ecosystem for Smart Growth Leaders

1. Listen to Whitney Johnson, "Embrace Constraints," *Disrupt Yourself* podcast, episode 140, December 10, 2019, https://whitneyjohnson.com/embrace-constraints/.

2. For more on prioritizing relationships and relatedness, listen to Whitney Johnson, interview with Aicha Evans, "Human Spirit and Technology," *Disrupt Yourself* podcast, episode 217, May 25, 2021.

3. For more on resilience, listen to *Disrupt Yourself* podcast episodes with Justin Osofsky, (episode 218), Embrace Constraints, (episode 140), and Give Failure Its Due, (episode 200).

Epilogue

1. Gabriel Tarde, *The Laws of Imitation* (Rahway, NJ: Henry Holt & Company, 1903), 127.

Index

Acknowledgments

The only true gift is a portion of thyself.

—RALPH WALDO EMERSON

Emerson captures how I feel as I write these acknowledgments to my colleagues, friends, and family who have given a portion of themselves to make this book possible.

To my mother, who has always modeled a love of learning and a deep desire to grow. One of my happiest childhood memories is of my mother taking my younger sister, Brooke, and me to a bookstore every Friday afternoon, and of her reading *A Wrinkle in Time* to us. Then there was that copy of Tony Robbins's *Awaken the Giant Within* that Mom gave me while I was in college . . .

I owe a huge debt of gratitude to Heather Hunt—writer extraordinaire, intellectual sparring partner (though I will never be her equal), truth teller, and longtime friend from our college days working in the Orem Public Library. And deep appreciation to Frank Morgan, who has a journalist's eye for detail and is a storyteller nonpareil.

Thank you to Scott Berinato, my editor at Harvard Business Press. Scott deftly edited the manuscript, making it more economical and more musical. His rendering of the S Curve is a thing of beauty. Thank you, Scott, for being a tireless sponsor and advocate, always seeking the win.

Appreciation also to Melinda Merino and Erika Heilman. Thank you for being willing to wrestle our way to making this a truly useful book. Thank you to Stephani Finks for the drop-dead gorgeous book cover, and to the production team, headed by Jen Waring and Jane Gebhart, for making the process easy. And always grateful for Julie Devoll, Felicia Sinusas, Jon Shipley, Sally Ashworth, and Claus Mossbeck for putting their heart and soul into getting my ideas out into the world. And thank you, always, Erika, for betting on my very first book, *Dare, Dream, Do*.

A special shout-out to Julie Berry, who helped me move up my S Curve of Learning as an author. I will forever be grateful to Julie for encouraging me to take the time I needed to make this the book I wanted it to be, and then for her deep-dive edit. This book is infinitely better for having been under Julie's watchful care. Thanks also to Sarah Green Carmichael, who gave the introduction a much-needed makeover (even if we did have to cut Uncle Rico).

Deep gratitude goes to Michael Bungay Stanier, who called one day and asked, "How can I help?" After lots of back and forth and countless iterations, we were still struggling with a title. Michael suggested we try *Smart Growth*. Having Michael devote a small portion of his intellectual wattage to me led to an unexpected and serendipitous reframing of the big idea. Then there's his sensory descriptor of the S Curve—"slow, fast, slow." That's how we grow.

Thank you to Kurt Wilson for refining the S Curve Insight Platform, with input from Eric Lin and Marla Gottschalk. And thanks to Heather Schafer for thinking through the complexities around IP. Thank you too to Kurt Wilson and Sue Barlow for helping make the end-of-chapter summaries work—repeating back to me what I thought I said. Appreciation to Chelsea Smith and Linda Elliott for navigating the scheduling twists and turns that come with writing a book. Thank you to the glue of our book launch team, Jen Ross, and our team of supporters, Amelia Atencio, Stephanie Brummel, and Nicole Pellegrino!

A special shout-out to Terry Sejnowski and Tara Swart, MD, for helping me puzzle out the neuroscience of the S Curve; to my husband, Roger Johnson, on the biology of the S Curve, and Juan C. Mendez, who a decade ago was invaluable in helping me think through how the S Curve could apply to people.

Thank you to my accountability partners, Eric Schurenberg and Harry Kraemer, for their weekly check-ins and for generously sharing their stories.

Thank you to Carol Kauffman, who read an early version of the manuscript and gave me expert guidance on how a coach would approach this. Carol is a walking encyclopedia on the literature of positive psychology.

Thank you to readers Alison Caldwell-Andrews, Angie Balfour, Brigham Doxey, Dallin Hunt, Darrell Rigby, David Nihill, Eric Lin, Harry Kraemer, Jason Jedlinski, Mary Jolley, Miranda Johnson, Monica Loup, Nancy Wilson, Paige Blaser, Spencer Combs, Stacey Johnson, and Sumeet Shetty. "Real craftsmanship reflects real caring," said Spencer W. Kimball. And I felt that from each of my readers.

Thank you to all who agreed to be interviewed on the *Disrupt Yourself* podcast and on LinkedIn Live. Many of these stories found their way into the book.

And thanks to those whose work influenced me as I was writing, including Jennifer Aaker and Naomi Bagdonas, Luvvie Ajayi Jones, Cesar Baez, Albert-Lazlo Barabasi, William Bridges, Brené Brown, Julie Carrier, Stephen M. R. Covey, Chris Dancy, Nancy Duarte, Malcolm Gladwell, Adam Grant, Heidi Grant, Marshall Goldsmith, Suneel Gupta, Charles Handy, Devanie Helman, Jeffrey R. Holland, Marcy Jellison, Dallas Jenkins, Steve Ludwig, Julie Lythcott-Haims, Emma McAdam, Kelly McGonigal, Alan Mulally, Russell M. Nelson, Scott Osman, Alex Osterwalder, Tom Peters, David Peterson, Dan Pink, Bob Proctor, Tom Rath, Richard Riso, Kim Scott, Ben Shewry, Jeff Slovin, Brooke Snow, Laura Vanderkam, and Isabel Wilkerson.

Thank you to those who so generously endorsed this book. Doing so is a gift of both time and personal credibility.

An especially huge thanks to Amy Humble, my business partner, for persuading me that this was the next book I needed to write and for thinking through the real-world application of these ideas. I am continually in awe of Amy's brilliant and strategic mind. When she puts her brain on something, and adds in her whole heart, there is real magic. I am grateful too to Amy Gray for connecting us—she is a blessing.

To my husband, Roger, who created an ecosystem where people can grow, especially me. To our children, David and Miranda, it is wonderful to be on the lily pad with you. And to God, from the deepest place in my being, thank you.

About the Author

WHITNEY JOHNSON (whitneyjohnson.com) is CEO of the human capital consultancy Disruption Advisors, one of Inc. 5000's fastest-growing private companies in America (2020). Named by Thinkers50 as one of the leading business thinkers in the world, Johnson is an expert at smart growth leadership: growing your people to grow your company.

Johnson is an award-winning author, a world-class keynote speaker, and a frequent lecturer for Harvard Business School's Corporate Learning. She has 1.8 million followers on LinkedIn, where she was selected as a Top Voice in 2020. Her course on Fundamentals of Entrepreneurship has been viewed more than one million times, and she hosts a weekly LinkedIn Live now nearing a cumulative million views. She also hosts the weekly *Disrupt Yourself* podcast, where her guests have included Brené Brown, Stephen M. R. Covey, John Mackey, and Mike Rowe.

An innovation and disruption theorist, Johnson is a frequent contributor to *Harvard Business Review* and *MIT Sloan Management Review*, as well as the author of the bestselling *Build an A-Team*, a *Financial Times* and 800-CEO-READ Book of the Month, and the critically acclaimed *Disrupt Yourself*. In these books, Johnson codifies the S Curve of Learning and the Seven Accelerants of Personal Disruption, which provide a systematic approach to leadership development.

Johnson was the cofounder, with Harvard Business School's Clayton Christensen, of the Disruptive Innovation Fund and is formerly an award-winning Wall Street stock analyst, where she was an Institutional Investor–ranked equity research analyst for eight years and rated by StarMine as a superior stock picker.

Johnson is married, has two children, and lives in Lexington, Virginia, where she and her family grow strawberries, raspberries, and blackberries and enjoy making jam.

. . .

If you've finished reading this book and would like more resources, go to disruptionadvisors.co/smartgrowthbook.

If you would like to learn more about how our team can be of help to you, email us at workwithus@whitneyjohnson.com.

If you would like to sign up for our weekly newsletter, go to disruptionadvisors.co/newsletter.

If you want to share how you are growing smarter because of this book, I would love to hear your story. Email me at wj@whitneyjohnson.com.